Paul König

Voyage of the Deutschland

The First Merchant Submarine

Paul König

Voyage of the Deutschland

The First Merchant Submarine

ISBN/EAN: 9783954272839
Erscheinungsjahr: 2013
Erscheinungsort: Bremen, Deutschland

© *maritimepress in Europäischer Hochschulverlag GmbH & Co. KG, Fahrenheitstr. 1, 28359 Bremen. Alle Rechte beim Verlag und bei den jeweiligen Lizenzgebern.*

www.maritimepress.de | office@maritimepress.de

VOYAGE OF THE
DEUTSCHLAND

CAPTAIN PAUL KÖNIG

From a photograph taken on the *Deutschland*
at Baltimore

VOYAGE OF THE
DEUTSCHLAND

THE FIRST MERCHANT SUBMARINE

BY

CAPTAIN PAUL KÖNIG

NEW YORK
HEARST'S INTERNATIONAL LIBRARY CO.
1916

CONTENTS

CHAPTER   PAGE

INTRODUCTION   ix

I. How Germany Got the *U-Deutsch-land*, and How the *U-Deutschland* Got Me   1

II. Trial Trip and Outward Bound . .   12

III. The First Day at Sea.   20

IV. The U-Boat Trap.   35

V. Head Downwards in the North Sea.   48

VI. Westward Ho!   61

VII. In the Atlantic   72

VIII. Hell With the Lid On.   109

IX. America.   121

X. Baltimore   136

XI. Farewell to Baltimore   160

XII. Breaking Through.   183

XIII. Homeward Bound   191

XIV. Home Again   211

XV. How Germany Welcomed Us Back .   218

[v]

„Zum Kämpfen und Streiten man rufet Euch nicht,
Zum friedlichen Handel führt Euch die Pflicht,
Glück auf denn! Gott mit Euch, er segne die Fahrt,
Seid wacker und mutig nach echt deutscher Art;
Dass wieder ihr kehrt in die Heimat zurück,
Ganz Deutschland Euch wünschet herzinniglich Glück!"

HEINRICH, PRINZ VON PREUSSEN.

HERRN KAPITÄN KÖNIG,
  dem Führer des ersten
  deutschen Handels-U-Bootes

ILLUSTRATIONS

FACING PAGE

Capt. Paul König. From a photograph taken on the
Deutschland at Baltimore .. .. *Frontispiece*
Capt. Paul König. From a photograph taken in
Bremen before the war 16
The *Deutschland* coming up Chesapeake Bay on the
way to Baltimore 17
The American manager of the German Ocean Navi-
gation Co., welcoming Captain König on his arrival
at quarantine, Baltimore 32
Posing for their first American photograph. A por-
tion of the crew on the stern of the *Deutschland*
on its way up Chesapeake Bay 33
The tug *Timmins* conveying the *Deutschland* from
quarantine to Baltimore 48
A three-quarter view from the stern of the *Deutschland* as she was warped into her berth at Baltimore 49
Preparing to dock at Baltimore. An exceptional
view from the stern showing unique construction.. 64
The *Deutschland* docking at Baltimore 65
Left—Captain Hinsch, of North German Lloyd. *Cen-
ter*—Capt. Paul König. *Right*—Paul G. L. Hilken,
American Manager German Ocean Navigation
Company 80
Ashore at Baltimore after many days at sea. First
picture of the crew of the *Deutschland* taken on
arrival 81
Capt. Paul König. Photograph taken in Baltimore
on arrival of the *Deutschland* 96
Paul G. L. Hilken, American Manager, German
Ocean Navigation Company 97
A close view of the commanding tower and periscope
of the *Deutschland* 112
The first autographed photograph in America after
the arrival of the *Deutschland*, signed by Captain
König, First Officer Krapohl, and Chief Engineer
Klees 113

Voyage of the Deutschland

FACING PAGE

The last photograph of the *Deutschland* leaving
Baltimore. The *Deutschland* as she appeared passing out to sea from Chesapeake Bay 128

The creators of the Submarine Mercantile Service.
Director Zetzmann, builder of the merchant submarine, *Deutschland*. Alfred Lohmann, founder of
the German Ocean Navigation Company.. 129

Up the Weser to Bremen. The *Deutschland* receiving
ovation on its triumphant return to Germany.. 142-143

A broadside view of the submarine 160

The *Deutschland* with all colors set, the German flag
at her fore-peak, the United States flag aft, approaching the mouth of the Weser 161

The triumphant return to Germany. The *Deutschland*
entering the mouth of the Weser 176

Home at last. The *Deutschland* alongside its pier
in Bremen 177

Welcoming the crew of the *Deutschland* at the City
Hall in Bremen 192

Captain König and Dr. Alfred Lohmann, President
of the German Ocean Navigation Company, leaving reception given Captain König in Bremen .. 193

Celebration at City Hall, Bremen, August 25, 1916.
The crowd in front numbered many thousands.
The officers and crew on the balcony acknowledging
cheers 208

Portrait of officers and crew of *Deutschland* taken
on their arrival at the mouth of the Weser, August
23, 1916 209

Interior view of the *Deutschland*. The central control or navigating room 224

The *Deutschland* on the stocks. Photograph taken
the day before launching 225

INTRODUCTION

THE mysterious voyage of the merchant submarine *Deutschland* has now kept the attention of the old and new world under strain quite long enough. The wildest rumors regarding our trip and our fate have cropped up in innumerable papers, not to mention the magnificent flights of fiction made by the English. We were stranded, we were sunk—we had even been taken apart and sent in separate packages to America. What fun we used to have on the high seas when our wireless operators would catch one of these plump English *canards* in full flight! I therefore have the greater pleasure in giving a longer, more detailed description of our legendary voyage and our adventures.

The voyage, after all, was far from being a fabulous one—for this would have made it doubly precarious. And as for adventures, we naturally avoided these as far as possible.

I hope, therefore, that the reader will not expect a whole series of exciting episodes, such as may fall to the lot of a military submarine in the war area. Our duty was as follows: to transport our valuable cargo to America as smoothly, and with as few interruptions as possible, to make a joke of the English blockade, and to return with a cargo equally valuable. These things we accomplished, and I shall now describe *how* we accomplished them.

That our voyage did not always proceed smoothly, that now and then we found ourselves in devilish hot water, that this or that did not come off according to program—was entirely owing to the gentle endeavors of the English. The reader owes them thanks for these little exciting interludes. The English, to be sure, despite all attempts, were unable to hinder our course—still they succeeded in giving additional color and variety to my account of it. It would be ungracious not to acknowledge this.

I wish to express my special thanks to my two officers of the watch, Messrs. Krapohl and Eyring. The notes taken by these two gentlemen completed my own on many points. It is impossible for a captain to remain continually on the turret—I had almost said "bridge" from old habit—and then six eyes see more than two. And to be able to see is one of the first laws of the submarine.

PAUL KÖNIG.

The Voyage of the Deutschland

I

HOW GERMANY GOT THE "U-DEUTSCHLAND," AND HOW THE "U-DEUTSCHLAND," GOT ME

How did Germany come to build the *U-Deutschland?* That would be a long story. I must leave it to others to relate—to men who are better qualified. The most important facts are revealed in the speeches which were made upon the return of the *Deutschland* during the festivities in honor of this history-making event at the Rathaus in Bremen. These may be read in the description I give of our reception at the close.

The idea of building submarine

cargo-boats for long distance is to me
an idea growing out of the resolve of
the German people to nullify the blockade of the German and American
coasts, as well as the complete cutting-
off of our legitimate imports. The
old Hanseatic spirit of enterprise, the
technical genius of German shipbuilding, and the efficiency of one of our
largest shipyards combined to give
British arrogance upon the seas the
heaviest blow it has suffered since the
Union Jack first fluttered over the
waves.

It is impossible to forecast to-day
what changes and revolutions will follow upon the building and traffic of
submarine merchant ships. It is possible that all the laws of naval warfare
may be altered. Through this the sum
and relationship of armed ships may

undergo change throughout the world, and this may influence the destiny of the nations even more than the present war. It would seem that humanity stood face to face with a new epoch of its history.

We Germans may well be proud of the fact that this epoch has been ushered in by a German ship. That Canadian war-submarines crossed the Atlantic before us cannot alter this truth. They traveled in groups, always upon the surface, and under escort of torpedo-boats, cruisers and auxiliary craft. Moreover, they traveled under far more favorable conditions than a merchant submarine, since they had only to carry their provisions and munitions and no dead weight apart from their armament. They were above all able to defend themselves.

On the other hand the sole means of defense of a submarine freighter consists in diving. And even this is not everywhere possible with a large vessel of over 2,000 tons.

I was therefore faced by a new and extraordinary problem when asked to navigate the *U-Deutschland* to America. The task would have been almost as novel had I been a young patrol-boat commander instead of an old Lloyd captain, and a navigator of big liners.

But I must first tell you how the *U-Deutschland* managed to requisition me. Things developed with great swiftness and many surprises.

I happened to be in Berlin during the middle of September, 1915, on some business or other. I had been forced to surrender my good ship *Schleswig*

long before, but the North German
Lloyd knew where it could find me.
One evening I found a message at my
hotel. It was from Herr Lohmann,
of Bremen, who asked me to come and
see him at the Adlon, in Berlin, as soon
as possible.

I was surprised. I knew, of course,
that Herr Lohmann was the head of
the well-known Bremen house, and I
had met him personally in Sydney,
where his firm had the agency of the
North German Lloyd.

But what did Herr Lohmann wish to
see me for *now—now* when "German
shipping had been swept from the
seas"—as you might read day after
day in any English paper? There
would be certain difficulties in starting
a new German line of steamers to Aus-
tralia or the Straits under present con-

ditions. As for the Baltic, I knew that his firm had no connections there. What could they want with an old East Asia—America—and Mediterranean sea-dog like myself?

Those thoughts went puzzling through my head as I made my way to the Adlon.

Herr Lohmann greeted me in the most affable manner. He did not beat long about the bush. After referring to the pleasant days in Sydney, he asked me if I was not bored by this uneventful sitting about on land? Was I not anxious to be up and off on—a long cruise?

What was an old captain of the merchant marine to say to that?—an old captain who had to leave his ship at the outbreak of war, and was drifting about the country like a derelict—

while the English cruisers were prowling about the Canal and the Shetlands and taking the American mails from neutral ships at four miles distance from New York?

I shrugged my shoulders and was silent.

Then the secret came out. Herr Lohmann now told me that he was entertaining the idea of running a line of submarine merchant ships between Germany and America. He asked me whether I was willing to navigate the first of these vessels? ' The first trip would be to Newport News. He knew that I had a certain amount of knowledge regarding the waters and soundings of Chesapeake Bay, acquired during my trips in the Baltimore service of the North German Lloyd. Did I think that I would be able to take a freight boat of this kind across to America—in case the thing really came off?

This was to the point. I have never been fond of long deliberations, so I promptly said: "Yes!"

Here was a chance for an old fellow, over 45, to take part in this war of "black lists" and daily mail robberies.

"Herr Lohmann," I said, "if the thing really comes off, I am your man!"

And the thing did come off!

In less than two months a telegram called me to Berlin to an important conference. Here I looked at sketches, plans and working drawings until my eyes swam. Four more months passed which I utilized to the full. I then went to Kiel and saw a remarkable framework of steel slowly take shape upon

the stocks across the way at Gaarden.
Rotund, snug and harmless the thing
lay there. Inside it were hidden all
the countless, complicated and powerful features of those sketches and
working drawings. I cannot boast that
the reality as executed in steel and
brass was any easier to grasp than the
endless network of lines and circles
which had bewildered me when inspect-
ing the blue-prints.

Those of you who have seen illustra-
tions and photographs of the interior
of the "central-station" or the "turret" of a submarine, will understand
what I mean. And should you have
entered a submarine itself and felt
yourself hopelessly confused by the bewildering chaos of wheels, vents,
screws, cocks, pipes, conduits, above,
below and all about—not to speak of

the mysterious levers and weird mechanisms, each of which has some important function to fulfil, you may find some consolation in the thought that my own brains performed a devils' dance at the sight.

But after this monster, with its tangle of tubes and pipes, had been duly christened, and its huge gray-green body had slid majestically into the water, it suddenly became a ship. It swam in its element as though born to it—as though it had never known another.

For the first time I trod the tiny deck and mounted the turret to the navigation platform. From here I glanced down and was surprised to see beneath me a long, slender craft—with gracious lines and dainty contours. Only the sides, where the green body vaulted massively above the water, gave an indication of the huge size of the hull. I felt pride and rapture as my eye took in this picture. The fabric swayed slightly beneath my feet —an impressive combination of power and delicacy.

And now I knew that what had at first seemed to me nothing more than the product of some mad phantasy on the part of the technicians was in reality a ship. It was a ship in which oceans might be crossed, a real ship, to which the heart of an old sailor like myself might safely attach itself.

I laid my hand upon the edge of the *U-Deutschland's* turret and pledged her my faith.

And thus I came to the *U-Deutsch-land* and became the commander of the first undersea merchant vessel.

[11]

II

TRIAL TRIP AND OUTWARD BOUND

WE were now in for a strange and wonderful time. Day after day we went out into the bights and down into the depths. We made trial trips in all sorts of weather and at every opportunity. Every man of our picked crew knew of the task we were expected to fulfil.

Our job was to acquire facility in steering this fine and complicated craft, the last word in bold and subtle computation. Our job was to learn how to understand and control this most marvellous product of modern shipbuilding, the submarine. We were obliged to learn how to impose our wills upon this heavy mass of almost 2,000 tons, so that it would obey the slightest turn of the rudder, and turn and manœuvre like a torpedo-boat, and rise and sink in the water like a dirigible in the air.

It was also necessary to observe the strength of the steel body, to test the force and obedience of the powerful engines, to study the imperfections or little perversities of the whole, to capture the secret of the life and movement of this weird, mysterious, fish-like organism.

A submarine is as full of moods as a woman, and as delicate as a race horse. It is as solid as a tramp steamer, and as reliable as a tug-boat. It may have good qualities—and bad. It may be as manageable as a racing yacht, or it may buck like a broncho, and it will only obey him who knows it from the beginning to the end of its minute mechanism.

So we spent weeks upon the seas— upon and beneath them. We studied our boat, and strove to grow acquainted with all its possibilities. We were bent on mastering *all* the peculiarities of this nautical amphibian.

After returning from the quiet bays and coves, where we carried on our practice, to the yards, the smashing uproar of the rivetting hammers and the ceaseless clamor of the docks, we would sit for hours with the constructors and swap experiences. Many hints and valuable suggestions resulted from this practical experience, and gave rise to new plans and ideas.

I cannot sufficiently express my thanks to these gentlemen—the shipbuilders who worked hand in hand with me. They never tired in their efforts to assist us, nor in helping to test this wonderful creation of their inventive genius. On the very day of our departure, Chief Engineer Erbach, the constructor of the vessel, rowed out to our anchorage—in order to make one final diving test.

* * *

The day of our departure had come. The *U-Deutschland* had been loaded. The precious cargo lay well packed in the freight-chambers. Then the whole ship was once more overhauled and brought to a perfect trim. We then stored enough provisions for this long trip; then came boxes of cigars, and gramophone plates.

All our various needs had been provided for and the *U-Deutschland* was ready to "sail."

We, too, were ready. Our farewells with our loved ones had already taken place, thank God—at home. These moments, especially when there is to be a trip into the unknown, are always painful ones, which had best be got over as quickly as possible. Our last handclasps were with the men of the Germania Shipyard.

Then the gang-plank was drawn in. I ordered the men to their stations and mounted the turret. The tug-boat *Charlotte* was already alongside and picked up the hawser. I called "Attention!" down into the central station and lifted my hand.

The mighty moment had come.

"Cast away aft!"

"Aye, aye, sir."

"Pull away, *Charlotte!*"

The bell of the signal dial upon the

CAPTAIN PAUL KÖNIG

From a photograph taken in
Bremen before the war

THE "DEUTSCHLAND" COMING UP CHESAPEAKE BAY ON THE WAY TO BALTIMORE

stout little tug-boat tinkles. The sturdy craft pulls the tow-line tight and slowly draws the stern of the *Deutschland* away from the wharf.

"Cast away for'd!"

"Aye, aye, sir."

The hawsers flop splashing from the pier wall into the grimy, churned-up water of the harbor.

And now it is our turn. I pick up the speaking-tube:

"Larboard engine—half power—reverse!"

"Starboard engine—slow speed ahead."

"Helm 20 points starboard!"

"Helm 20 starboard!"

The answers from the engine-room came up promptly.

From where I stood upon the turret, close beside the helmsman with his small wheel, I could scarcely feel the throb of the electric engines going into action. Only the dirty water, which was cast up by the propellers and went wallowing and whirling to sternward over the round body of the *Deutschland,* betrayed the fact that the engines were in operation.

Slowly the great green whale-back swung around and lay at first at right angles to the course, drove forward a little to larboard, remained still, and then pushed itself with the help of the tug once more to starboard stern on.

I ordered both engines to stop.

The boat still proceeded backwards for a piece, tugging fiercely at the towing cable like some cumbrous monster of the brine.

I cast a swift glance from the turret upon the course and the pier. There was now enough room to manœuvre in.

I ordered the tow-lines to be cast off and both engines to drive ahead at half speed with helm to larboard.

We were still turning and made a good clearance of the pier wall close to a large gray war-submarine which was just being completed. I then ordered the helm to be put amidships, and both engines:

"Full steam ahead!"

The bows of the ship began to tremble in rhythmic vibrations under the increased pressure from the engines. The water came foaming from the propellers. We were under way and the *Deutschland* began pushing herself faster and faster through the dingy waters of the port—out of the bay, out toward the broad ocean—toward the freedom of the seas.

III

THE FIRST DAY AT SEA

The North Sea came rolling toward us in long swells. The weather was bright and there was a stiff breeze Nor'-nor'-west. I stood with the First Officer of the Watch in the turret—in the "bath-tub." This is what we called the protecting wall of metal which rose above the navigation platform as a kind of parapet and encircled the turret manhole in elegant sweeping lines. It somewhat resembled the gondola of an aeroplane. The outer steering wheel is situated directly in front of this, but can be used only in fair weather.

We were standing in oilskins behind the shield, for the sea had just enough movement to wet everything. The deck was continually flooded and every few moments the waves went slapping against the turret. In my hand I held the speaking-tube connection with the central station, where the helmsman passes on the orders to the engineer by means of the signal dial. I stood with every sense alert. There was a sound of dull thumping, the bows plunged into the foam, the seas came rumbling across the deck and shot hissing up against the superstructure of the turret. The turret manhole had to be flung to instantly and we were forced to duck behind the protecting wall in our crackling oilskins. These manœuvers were repeated every few minutes.

In the intervals we rose to a standing position, listened to the howling of the wind, and gazed at the horizon. The

German coast toward the southeast had vanished behind us some time before and the only bit of the homeland still with us was the accompanying torpedo-boat which was forging on ahead of us. We soon approached the outermost chain of German foreposts. Four patrol vessels passed us in a keel line and hoisted the signal:

"Glückliche Reise!" (Bon Voyage!)

Our faithful escort then darted up closer to us. Her crew gave us three tremendous cheers, her officers stood at salute upon her bridge, and we two lonely men upon the turret returned the salute. Then the black craft struck her nose into a sea, made a splendid turning and drove off with a whirling wake. She grew smaller and smaller and then vanished with her fluttering pennons of smoke.

We were now left to ourselves. We were travelling into the unknown.

However, there was little time for meditation. Danger threatened us from all sides. I had to make sure that the craft was in the best of trim and that the engines and diving arrangements were under complete control.

I gave the order:

"Clear for a diving test!"

Instantly the response came back from the turret and the central station, and the men hurried to their posts. The oil engines were still hammering away at a mad rate. I left the alarm bell clang and jumped into the manhole of the turret. The cover was battened down, the engines stopped at the same moment.

We felt a slight pressure in our ears for a moment. We were cut off from outside and silence reigned. But this silence was merely an illusion—and was due to the change.

"Open the diving-valves. Submerge!"

The valves were flung open and the compressed air escaped hissing from the tanks. At the same time a gigantic, intermittent snorting ensued, like the blowing and belching of some prehistoric monster. There was an uncomfortable pressure in our ears, then the noise became more regular, followed by a buzzing and a shrill hum. All the high notes of the engines in the central station intermingled and made a bewildering noise. It was like a mad, diabolical singsong. And yet it was almost like silence after the dull, heavy pounding of the oil-motors—only more insistent and irritating. The penetrating hum in the various vents announced the fact that the diving mechanism was in operation. It moaned and sang lower and lower in the scale of tones. These slowly diminishing and steadily deepening tones give one the physical feeling of mighty volumes of water pouring in and flooding full.

You have the sensation of growing heavier and sinking as the boat grows heavier and sinks, even though you may not be able to see through the turret window, or the periscope, how the bows are gradually submerged and the water climbs higher and higher up the turret until all things without are wrapped in the eerie twilight of the depths.

The faithful lamps burned, however, and then a real silence suddenly ensued. There was no sound but the gentle, trembling rhythm of the electric engines.

I then gave the order:

"Submerge to twenty meters!"

"Both engines half steam ahead!"

I was able to follow our submersion by means of the manometer. Through flooding the tanks, the boat is given several tons over-weight and the enclosed ship's space is made heavier than the displaced quantity of water. The titanic fish, therefore, began to sink downward in its element, that is to say, it began, in a certain sense, to fall. At the same time the electric engines are put into motion and the propulsive force of the propellers acts upon the diving rudders and causes the sinking to become a gliding. After the required depth has been reached—something which may easily be read from the

manometer that records the depth—all
further sinking may be stopped by
simply lightening the hull, which is
done by forcing out some of the water
in the submarine's tanks. The furious
growling of the pump is always a sure
sign that the required depth is being
approached. The noise ceased, only the
electric motors continued to purr and
the word came from the central station:

"Twenty meters—even keel!"

"Rudder set!"

So we forged ahead at a depth of
20 meters. Of course we are "blind"
under such conditions and can regulate
our movements only by means of the
depth recorder and that precious little
jewel of the boat, our compass. No
ray of light reached us any longer from
without, the periscope was submerged
long ago and the steel safety covers

over the windows were closed. We had been metamorphosed completely into a fish.

Reports now came from all parts of the U-boat—the central, the engine-room, the bow, the stern, the cargo-room, the battery-room—all tight. The *Deutschland* might safely proceed through the deeps. But it is not always so simple a matter to steer a boat of this size at a specified depth. A change in the specific gravity of water in consequence of alterations in the temperature of the water or the amount of salt influences this greatly. As an example let me explain the difference between the water of the Baltic and that of the North Sea. The specific gravity of the two seas is in the relation of 1.013 to 1.025. This appears trifling. But with a boat of the size of

the *Deutschland,* which requires over-
weight of many tons to enable it to
dive, this difference mounts up to a
quite formidable weight. In order to
submerge in the denser water of the
North Sea, we must make our boat at
least 17 tons heavier than is necessary
in the Baltic—otherwise we cannot
dive. In addition, the most disagreeable surprises are to be expected whenever there are sudden alterations in the
temperature of the water, as in bays
and river mouths. These are further
influenced by the lighter sweet water.
Many a U-boat commander has been
misled by thinking that a certain over-
weight was all that was required to
take him under water and keep him
posed at a certain level. . . . Suddenly,
however, the manometer indicates a
still greater depth and the submarine

begins to fall like an aeroplane which has struck an "air-hole." A test of the specific gravity and the temperature of the water will usually explain such behavior on the part of the U-boat. Only calculations such as these will enable the commander of an undersea boat to sink into the depths and rise to the surface with a certain degree of assurance.

We had now completed our trial dive to my satisfaction. Everything was safe and in good working order—we had excellent control of our complicated apparatus.

I then gave the order to rise. The diving rudders were slanted "up" and soon I was able to observe their action and that of our gallant exhaust pump by the manometer.

After I had made sure that there were no vibrations from propellers to be heard in the vicinity and no steamer with which one might collide, we mastered the so-called "blind moment." This is the interval during which the boat has already risen so high as to permit of its being rammed, the while it is still too far under water to permit the use of the periscope above the surface to have a look around.

This interval is very brief. I stood at the eye-piece of the tube and stared hard. The field of vision grew lighter, silver air-bubbles rose glimmering, a winking of light and a rilling of water flashed athwart the glass, then daylight came—a picture appeared. Clear and luminous the North Sea lay outspread before me into the empty and endless horizon.

I then gave orders to rise to our full extent. The planes of the rudders forced the boat more and more toward the surface of the water. In order to accelerate this, compressed air was forced into one of the tanks. The movement was now very rapid, the turret cleared itself, the deck lifted itself dripping, the manhole in the turret was opened and fresh air came streaming in:

"Blow out the tanks!" was my next order.

There was a wild howling and hissing in the central station. The powerful air-blasts were forcing the water out of the diving tanks. This takes but a short time. As soon as one tank is empty, the air which has been blown into it comes bubbling up with a gurgling noise along the sides of the boat, which soon attains its normal position.

We were still proceeding under elec-

© Int. Press Exchange

THE AMERICAN MANAGER OF THE GERMAN OCEAN NAVIGATION CO. WELCOM-
ING CAPTAIN KÖNIG ON HIS ARRIVAL AT QUARANTINE, BALTIMORE

POSING FOR THEIR FIRST AMERICAN PHOTOGRAPH

A portion of the crew on the stern of the *Deutschland* on its way up Chesapeake Bay

tric power. The next step was to switch on the heavy Diesel motors by means of the electric engines. I had already climbed up to the turret and so I noticed nothing of this operation, except the reports that came to me from the central. But on such occasions an exciting picture is presented to the men in the engine-room.

The engine observers stand at their posts. The order comes through the speaking-tube—everybody is rigid with attention. Then the Chief Engineer gives a shrill whistle and lifts one hand. A few swift movements of the trained hand—and certain long and blinding lightnings flash across the switchboard in the electric-motor chamber. The first piston-heads lift themselves hesitatingly, slowly, unwillingly—then increase their speed. Terrific reports and loud hissings ensue, and a curious, irregular coughing. The roaring of the explosions then becomes rhythmic and faster and faster the engines fall into their places and begin to pulsate in a regular harmony—like the strokes of innumerable hammers.

The trial dive was at an end, and stamping and pounding, the *Deutschland* hurried on her way. The wind did not slacken, but the weather remained fair and observation was easy.

No steamer hove in sight—so we were able to proceed quietly on the surface. Of course we had the best of reasons for navigating with the utmost care and attention. Thus the day came to an end.

But when the sun sank in dull and threatening clouds, there was a storm brewing for the morrow.

IV

THE U-BOAT TRAP

AND there *was* a storm. The farther we left the coast behind, the more violent grew the sea. Our ship was flung and tossed about in great style. I was aware of this as I lay in my berth. About two o'clock in the morning I was awakened by a "Hoo—ee!" in the speaking-tube in the wall close to my head.

Second Officer of the Watch Eyring reported that a white light was visible to starboard and was swiftly approaching. I leaped out of my berth, went balancing around the corner into the central, then up the ladder, through the manhole and on to the platform.

Eyring pointed out a white light. It

was comparatively close and appeared to be coming on at a great rate. We decided to take no risks, sounded the alarm and dived. It was then that I felt for the first time that overwhelming sensation of security which arises from the possibility of such a rapid mode of escape.

It all seemed most natural. Here we were in the very midst of a world-war, going on our way with an unarmed freight-boat in the dead of night. A light draws near—it may be an enemy, most probably it *is* an enemy. In a few moments a couple of guns may flash forth, a couple of shells smash our superstructure, the seas go plunging into the inner shell of our craft and then the North Sea closes above our heads.

But nothing of this sort happened.

A brief command shot down to the central station. A few quick movements were made with hand-wheels or levers and we proceeded on our way in absolute safety. Brute force may bar our path upon the surface of the seas, but it is impotent and must let us pass as soon as we take our course a few yards under the surface.

For reasons of safety we continued to screw our way forward in a submerged state, and remained under water until dawn. We rose to the surface about four o'clock. It was already day, but unfortunately, there was a mighty uncomfortable sea running. We saw a few fishing boats in the distance, laboriously toiling away. We kept a sharp eye on them, but soon became convinced of their harmless character and so continued our course above water.

This was rough work. The movements of the submarine were such that the heads and stomachs of the men in the interior of the boat—which could only be ventilated by the fans—began to be affected. A part of the crew found no charm in the temptations of dinner. It was also impossible to remain on deck, since this was constantly being flooded. It was a trifle dryer behind the protecting wall of the "bath-tub" and in the lee of the turret, protected from the sea and the wind. Here a few members of the free watch remained huddled. They clutched the rails, sniffed up the fresh air, and shook themselves whenever a breaker came bursting against the turret in an eruption of foam and spray.

We proceeded thus during the entire day. We saw a few steamers in the distance—as betrayed by their smoke; but these we avoided by a change of course above water after carefully getting their bearings and observing what course they were following.

This is not so difficult as would appear. You know your own bearings and can obtain those of the other vessel by triangulation and computing its position and course by means of the chart. After comparing these details with the lines of the chief steamer routes as marked in the charts, you are able to tell with a fair degree of certainty in what direction the steamer must be travelling.

A computation of this sort, as luck would have it, happened to prove of the greatest importance to us shortly after, and—as you shall see—it was even in the nature of a certain amount of documentary evidence.

Toward evening the weather had cleared a little, and even the sea had grown quieter. The sun went down amidst beautifully illuminated clouds.

The entire watch had come up to get a breath of fresh air and to light up a cigar or cigarette. Smoking below decks is strictly forbidden. The men all crowded closely together, over and under each other, against the protected side of the turret, hugging the steel wall. They made a remarkable picture in their rough and heavy sea clothes and looked like a swarm of bees—a grape-like cluster of tangled human forms. Not much etiquette was observed to be sure. I let the men do as they pleased. Their job was a hard one down below. When one of them wished to stick his head out of the manhole in order to have a few whiffs of his pipe, I gladly granted him the brief enjoyment.

All eyes were now engaged in searching the horizon. This was a good thing, for the more eyes there are peeled the more the ship sees. Some of the men had eyes like hawks.

We saw two masts come bobbing up to port in the translucent twilight of this June evening. A smoke-stack followed and soon the hull of a steamer loomed above the horizon. With the aid of our powerful prism-glasses we were able to keep her under close observation. We decided to fix her course, so as to be able to avoid her, yet remain on the surface. We soon managed to secure a few good observations and I proceeded to consult the chart. I studied this, made comparisons, took another observation, made certain calculations and once again referred to the chart. I was stunned. The course this steamer was taking would never lead her into any port!

How could this be possible?

She was steering directly for the coast—heading for the rocks!

I summoned Krapohl and showed him my figures. We once more took the steamer under observation with our glasses and compared the chart— everything tallied. The fellow was bound straight for nothingness!

In the meantime we had approached close enough to enable us to distinguish her clearly. The June evening was still so clear and bright that we could remark everything with great ease.

She was a fine steamer, of middling size, carried a large neutral flag and was conspicuously painted with the same colors along her sides. In the middle of her length she bore a long, double name, which we could not yet make out.

Suddenly Kropohl sang out:

"Donnerwetter! how does it happen that this fellow is still flying his colors so long after sundown? Can that be mere accident? And there's something suspicious about the way that paint is laid on! The rascal looks queer to me!"

I was forced to agree. I was particularly suspicious about the senseless course the ship was taking. One doesn't go promenading for pleasure around the reaches of the North Sea in the midst of a World War!

We consulted as to what action to take. The steamer apparently had not yet seen us. She pursued her mysterious course and was already a trifle off our stern.

I therefore decided not to dive, since our two courses would soon take us far apart.

Suddenly the steamer made a sharp turn and came directly toward us. We were now able to see that this good neutral had also swung out his boats, naturally in order to establish still further his character as a harmless merchantman who was ready for all contingencies and quite willing to obey all the orders of a fighting submarine.

We were sufficiently satisfied with this most ingratiating endeavor to please. I sent all men below decks and at once sounded the alarm. We pre-

pared to dive and made a turn toward
the steamer, so as to lie cross to the
seas, as this facilitates getting under
water.

And now to our great astonishment,
we observed the following: The neutral steamer had hardly seen us make
one turn and prepare to dive, than she
made a quick move and altered her
course. And as we sank beneath the
surface we saw her vomiting clouds of
smoke and making for the distance in
a zigzag course!

This confession of an uneasy con-
science was overwhelming evidence for
us. We roared with laughter over the
flight of this jolly "neutral" with the
mysterious course. The crafty fellow
knew that the game was up. He naturally took us for a war submarine and
was fearful of getting a torpedo be-

[45]

tween his ribs during the next few moments.

He must have been boiling with rage. It would have been so pleasant to come up close to the "pest" under the guise of a "neutral" and then at a safe distance to drop his porthole covers and his harmless colors and to let fly at us with shells. The U-boat trap had been prettily prepared—the German "pirate" need only have come a trifle closer!

Instead of accommodating our friend the enemy, we made our bow under water and emerged after some two hours had elapsed. I first searched the horizon through the periscope and then, still half submerged, I opened the turret manhole in order to sweep the seas with the glass. All was safe. The moon had risen in the south, and made the bright summer night still more radiant. As far as my vision reached, the sea was clear, not a steamer in sight.

The *Deutschland* might now go her ways unhindered. Apart from the joy felt over the disillusionizing of the cunning manipulator of the U-boat trap, I now had the certitude that we would be able to see all vessels before they saw us.

That, as you will agree, is, under the circumstances, a great deal.

V

HEAD DOWNWARDS IN THE NORTH SEA

I HAD decided to proceed submerged under electric power during the darkest hours of the following night—that is, between eleven and one o'clock. When we made our dive during the dusk of the long summer day, there was still little wind. But a high swell was flowing—a sure sign that in a few hours the storm would come lashing along. About two o'clock A.M. I gave orders to rise and was soon aware, by the increasingly wild movements of the boat, that the storm had come and that a still heavier sea was accompanying it.

Our craft made regular leaps and capers. Nevertheless we calmly blew

THE TUG "TIMMINS" CONVEYING THE "DEUTSCHLAND" FROM QUARANTINE TO BALTIMORE

A Three-quarter View from the Stern of the "Deutschland" as She Was Warped Into Her Berth at Baltimore

out our tanks and came up in fine fashion. As soon as the periscope projected, I tried to obtain a view of things above. But it was impossible to see a thing, as the periscope cut into thick hills of water every few moments. In addition to this the cold, gray dawn light made the waves that came wallowing along appear still larger and more sinister than usual. So we emerged completely above the surface. I climbed upon the turret, in order to have a proper look over the madly waltzing seas.

A pretty bit o' weather! All around us in the livid glow of the dawn a veritable witch's kettle of impossibly monstrous mountains of water crowned with foam, which the wind blew off in the shape of briny dust and drove hissing through the air. The boat labored heavily head on, and now and again fell violently away. The entire deck was, of course, flooded. Every few seconds a sea came lurching against the turret and burst over me in dense showers of spray. I clung to the parapet of the "bath-tub" and searched the horizon— a most remarkable horizon of heavy hills of water which went sliding in and out like the wing-pieces in a stage-setting.

I was just about to order the Diesel engines to be switched on—when I gave a start. What was *that*—that dark line there? Was it a trail of smoke?

But it was already blocked out by a billow which shoved itself between the ashen heavens and the heaving sea. . . .

I watched and waited, and stared through my glass until my eyes began to ache. . . .

There it was again! No doubt of it
—it *was* a glimmer of smoke; and
there!—thin as a needle—a masthead!
I had got it centered in my glass. And
then! as I bored my eyes into the glass
—something came heaving up out of
the valleys of the sea—a dark, drab
thing—with smoke hanging above it—
and four squat smoke-stacks . . .

"*Donnerwetter*—a destroyer!"

I made one jump into the turret and
slammed the cover fast.

"Alarm! Dive quickly! Flood!"

"Set diving rudder!"

"Twenty meters depth!"

The commands were uttered in almost one breath. But the execution of
them!

To attempt to dive with such a sea
running was sheer madness, as experience has taught us. What was I to do?

The destroyer might have seen us already!

Well, we knew we must get under—and as quickly as possible.

The men in the central below me were working away in silent haste. All the exhausts were opened wide, the compressed air hissed from the tanks —the diving vents were chanting in all possible keys.

I stood with my lips pressed together and stared out of the turret window upon the tossing sea, and watched for the first sign of our going down. But our deck remained still visible and we were continually lifted into the air by some wave. There was not a moment to be lost.

I ordered the diving rudder to be set still more sharply and both engines to drive ahead with full power.

The whole vessel quivered and thrilled under the increased pressure of the engines and made several leaps. She staggered about in the furious seas—but still seemed loath to leave the surface. Then she gave a jerk and her bows suddenly dipped and cut into the flood. She began to sink into the depths at an ever-increasing angle. The coming daylight vanished from the windows of the turret, the manometer in rapid succession showed 2—3—6— 10 meters depth. But the angle of the boat also began to increase.

We staggered about, leaned back, slipped off our feet. We then lost our footing entirely—for the floor of the *Deutschland* slanted sharply toward the front. I was just able to catch hold of the ocular or eye-piece of the periscope. Down in the central the

[53]

men were hanging on to the hand-wheels of the diving rudder. A few terrible seconds passed thus.

We had not yet seized the full significance of this new situation when there came a severe shock. We were hurled to the floor and everything that was not fastened down went flying in all directions.

We found ourselves in the queerest attitudes—and stared into one another's faces. There was a grim silence for a moment, then First Officer Krapohl remarked dryly:

"Well, we seem to have arrived!"

This broke the ghastly tension.

We were all rather pale around the gills, but at once tried to get our bearings.

What had happened?

What had caused this unnatural inclination of the boat? And why were the engines above us raving at intervals in a way that made the whole boat roar from stem to stern?

Before any of us had arrived at any solution of the mystery, our Chief Engineer, little Klees, had jumped up from his crouching position and, swift as lightning, had swept the engine-signal dial around to "Stop!"

And suddenly there was a deep silence.

We slowly assembled our proper legs and arms and thought hard over what had happened.

The vessel had slanted down toward the bows at an angle of about 36 degrees. She was standing, so to speak, on her head. Our bow was fast upon the bottom of the sea—our stern was still oscillating up and down like a mighty pendulum. The manometer showed a depth of about 15 meters.

I soon had a clear picture of our situation—it was far from cheering.

According to the chart we should have some 31 meters depth at this spot. But the steep slant of the long vessel must have caused the stern to go raking above the surface for a considerable distance. This would furnish a splendid target for an enemy destroyer. As long as the engines still ran, the following must also have occurred: Every time the hollow of a wave raced over us, the propellers raced in empty air part of the time, and no doubt increased our powers of attraction by flinging up fountains of water and whirls of foam. Klees had at once recognized this by the racing of the motors, and his presence of mind had at least obviated the more immediate peril.

Nevertheless we had betrayed our resting-place by a self-made little storm. And so we expected to hear the crash of a shell at any moment—smashing into the high-uprearing and outstanding stern overhead.

More seconds passed—under a terrific strain.

But nothing happened. The screws were no longer able to betray us. It was not yet full daylight overhead, and it was possible that the furious sea gave the destroyer enough to bother about.

Of course we at once hastened to get out of this idiotic fix. The boat had remained quite watertight, and had sustained the heavy shock without the slightest damage. So everything proceeded according to program. The after-tanks which had not yet been entirely exhausted of air were swiftly flooded, and so bit by bit the boat began to assume a more reasonable attitude.

Still she by no means lay horizontal as yet—for she had struck her nose too deeply into the mud for that. Nevertheless we were now completely under water and could proceed quietly with our work. The forward tanks were emptied of a part of their contents. Thus by balancing and trimming with the tanks we finally managed to get the bows clear of the bottom. We now began to rise, but were at once obliged to offset the inclination to oscillate caused by the full aft-tanks. After a time the center of gravity was again restored and I once more had the *Deutschland* well in hand.

We now also had time to consider what had caused this sudden bucking on the part of our usually so well-behaved boat? This must have been due to a whole chain of circumstances. Quite apart from the difficulty of submerging a large submarine in a high-running sea, it was possible that the tanks, owing to the haste induced by the presence of the destroyer, had not been quite freed of air. Added to this must be the sudden dynamic force exerted by the diving rudder, which in combination with the full force of the engines and the crushing weight of a particularly heavy sea, had given the boat this dangerous slant.

We were in a position similar to that of a dirigible balloon which steers for the earth at too steep an angle just before landing, and which is furthermore crushed to the ground with double force owing to a sudden downward blast of air. Of course, the wonderful material of our steel outer hull withstood the shock without damage. It is, however, possible that the bottom of the North Sea sustained some slight damage in latitude x degrees north, and in longitude x degrees east.

One thing appears remarkable to me, as I now strive to recollect what my impressions were as we rushed at full speed downward into the depths at an angle of 36 degrees—my first thoughts were entirely for the cargo. Was it well stored? Might it not be pitched about? This thought was wholly instinctive, odd as this may seem, for the Old Adam which has once got hold of the captain of a big fat liner is not easily shaken off, even when he steps aboard a submarine.

VI

"WESTWARD HO!"

We had had enough of the North Sea. And now we were about to strike for the outer reaches—for the "open sea!"

As to our course, everything, thank Heaven, was certain! Less certain, to be sure, were the things that might happen to us upon that course. We were bound to encounter various little surprises.

But what is the use of voyaging in a submarine if you are not ready to evade surprises—and to evade them with a good chance of success? We thought of the numbers of war subma- rines which had been successful in reaching the outer seas. And these fighting brethren of ours had a certain number of difficult duties to fulfil *en route*—whereas we had merely to avoid being seen, and to slip through with a whole hide.

The first duty imposed upon us was, of course, not so much to avoid being seen, as to avoid being recognized as a merchant U-boat.

The peculiar nature of our gallant little *Deutschland* as an unarmed, peaceful merchant vessel would not have protected us a moment from being sunk instantly without warning. Of this we were absolutely convinced, and we were afterwards confirmed in this belief by the official declarations of the English and French governments.

Had they, however, recognized us as

a merchant submarine—then we should not only have been in immediate peril, but our entry into our American port of destination would have been endangered in the highest degree—for we should at once have had a pack of bloodthirsty sleuths lowering for our trail. Even if things went favorably, we should have been done out of the effect of our astonishing arrival in America. As you may well imagine, it was especially upon this point that we had set our pride and honor.

Such, in the main, were my deliberations, as we approached the regions of the "danger zone."

We "snaked" ourselves along with the greatest possible vigilance. We saw many things; we ourselves were seen but seldom, and recognized never. In the daytime we avoided various steamers by simply altering our course. During the night-time we drove along with all lights blinded, and dived whenever we thought it necessary.

The weather was also favorable. Once we sighted a British auxiliary cruiser at a considerable distance. She was bound in a definite direction, and was following a zigzag course. For a time we maintained a parallel course, keeping her under close observation. But the high seas that were running seemed to absorb her entire attention, and so we ourselves remained unobserved.

On another occasion, toward dusk, a ·patrol boat approached us. It had seen us and adopted the mask of harmlessness in order to tempt us to an attack. But we continued quietly on our way and the patrol boat gave up in

PREPARING TO DOCK AT BALTIMORE

An exceptional view from the stern, showing **unique construction**

THE "DEUTSCHLAND" DOCKING AT BALTIMORE

disgust. There were also swifter patrol craft which we were able to steer clear of in good time.

Later the wind subsided, and it began to grow misty. We dived and lay upon the bottom. There was no need of hurry, and why should we not grant ourselves a little rest?

The waters we chose were, to be sure, far from shallow—on the contrary, they were quite deep. But we reposed all the more safely and quietly for that. And we had a profound faith in the splendid sounding apparatus, and the wonderful compression hull of our good *Deutschland*.

This night, spent upon the bottom of the sea, meant real recuperation for all of us. We were all able to have a proper wash and to lie down to rest without having to fear that a sudden

"Hoo-ee!" in the speaking-tube would startle us out of our dreams. First, however, we had dinner—a real and regular dinner. The two gramophones were set going and we clinked our glasses, filled—thanks to somebody's thoughtful courtesy — with French champagne.

Our steward, Stucke—the dear soul! —served us with a solemn ceremoniousness, just as though he were still the dining-room steward aboard the *Kronprinzessin Cecilie,* and had not spent almost a year in French captivity! And now he was showing his arts aboard the *Deutschland* at a depth of many meters! He was inexhaustible in constantly devising new resources for our cheerful little mess, and it was amazing to see what undreamed-of quantities of silver and linen he was able to stow away in his miniature pantry and a couple of drawers.

The following morning we once more rose to the surface. The exhaust pumps snored and hummed, and we began to climb out of the depths with hundreds of gallons "above normal," and with the diving rudders set as they should go.

At a depth of twenty meters, the boat began to lose her fine stability. She rocked and tossed. The manometer was the first to record this, then the diving rudders began to announce the fact by setting up a stout resistance. They have a habit under such circumstances of bucking heavily.

The higher we rose, the more lively our movements grew. A very respectable sea was bowling along overhead.

I ordered us to proceed for a time

with the periscope protruding just above the surface and surveyed the field. Nothing could be seen but a waste of white-crested waves racing along. But this sort of weather was quite to my liking, for it enabled us to slide along without keeping up such a vigilant watch.

So I decided to emerge completely and ordered compressed air to be shot into the tanks until the turret was sufficiently free. Then the Diesel motors were switched on, and the ventilating mechanism began to supply fresh air. But we had no sooner opened the cover of the manhole than the first damp greetings came whizzing into the central. So we clamped her down again. Another tank was blown clear—the "turbo" blast made short work of the imprisoned water.

A certain trick of seamanship was, however, necessary, before we could undertake this step. In order to rise entirely it is necessary to lie in the trough of the waves, since a high sea makes it impossible for the long and heavy hull to emerge head on.

So under a low speed, we laid the *Deutschland* cross to the seas. She rolled heavily—a beastly situation! which almost shook the soul out of one's body. Every few moments the ponderous cross seas went rolling over the vessel. But she obeyed the diving rudders and slowly stuck her nose out of the water. After we had reached the surface the turret, with its periscopes, described terrifying arcs, swinging back and forth.

There was another highly unpleasant moment to get over—to bring the

Deutschland around upon her course once more.

I stood behind the thick turret windows down which the driving spray went steadily streaming, and braced myself with arms and legs against both sides in order to withstand the fearful tossing. Following old seaman's lore I watched for the period of irregular comparative calm, which usually follows upon three particularly tall waves.

The third billow had just lumbered by. I shouted an order to the helmsman in the central — the manœuvre succeeded. The bow slowly nosed itself around—and we resumed our old course without being specially hard pounded by the big rollers.

But there was still much work to do. The storm was still on the increase, and we were able to proceed only slowly against this heavy sea. In addition, some of the crew were suffering from seasickness, for the short jerky motions of the ship were dreadful.

But the farther we proceeded the more the long steady swell of the Atlantic became recognizable. The short plunging and thumping ceased and passed over into a slow majestic cradling swing. In the distance we observed two English cruisers returning homeward from some nightly cruise. We were lying too deep, however, for them to observe us, and we saw them disappearing rapidly in an opposite course.

We were now free of the English patrol boats. We steered joyously toward the west, out upon the vast and rolling Atlantic—toward freedom.

VII

IN THE ATLANTIC

WE were now safely upon the high seas. But the Atlantic was far from giving us a friendly welcome. We had become inured to many things during the last few days, but I was anxious to spare the nerves of my men. It was necessary to husband their strength as far as possible in view of the long voyage before us. So I decided to adopt a more southerly course, thinking to find better weather there. Unfortunately we were deceived in this.

As I now look over my log-book written during those first few days in the Atlantic, I constantly come across notes such as: "A heavy sea." "Stiff

wind from the west-nor'-west—velocity
8." "The wind develops to a storm."
"Heavy seas sweep over the entire boat
and even the turret." "The boat is
traveling under water almost the entire time." The few disconnected
phrases may give you some idea of the
serious and extraordinarily wearing
life of twenty-nine human beings in a
closed-in steel fish which cuts its way
without pause through a wild and
tumultuous sea.

Here, during these storms upon the
Atlantic, the splendid seaworthiness
and marvellous constructive genius em-
bodied in the *Deutschland* were put to
the most extreme tests. The elements
certainly did their utmost to defeat our
attempt to reach America. The most
terrific strain was put upon both the
hull of our boat and the engines, which

were forced to keep running at a regular speed day after day if we were to have any chance of reaching our goal.

I consider it an honorable obligation at this point to express my grateful thanks to the builders whose work had furnished us such a magnificent instrument for the successful completion of our voyage. It is easy to grow enthusiastic over a splendid ship which lies snug in some port and captivates everybody with its beautiful lines, or arouses the admiration both of sailors and landsmen as it goes rushing along at its highest speed, but the real worth of a ship, its inner worth, so to speak, can only be ascertained after it has stood its test upon the high seas. You realize its good qualities and have confidence in its reliability and seaworthiness only after it has made headway against a wind pressure of 10, and a sea of 8 degrees of velocity! And this not merely for a few hours, but for days and weeks! A ship has a good chance of proving her worth under *such* conditions.

This applies particularly to a U-boat in times of war. A tramp steamer in times of peace, a craft which is often able to fulfil all kinds of demands made upon it, is always able to reach some port in case of need, or to call for help. At the very worst, it can drive before the wind for a few days, and wait for better weather. But all this is impossible for the U-boat. In addition to the dangers of the sea, it must reckon with danger from the side of the enemy—the cruellest and most merciless of all enemies. There is no port of distress open to it. Should it remain helpless upon the surface only a few hours and be discovered, then every passing sail, which would be the first to bring help to a steamer in distress, will merely proceed to call to lowering bloodhounds of the sea to fall upon their prey. The master of no ship is so lonely, so forced to depend entirely upon himself as the master of a submarine. Should he not be able to depend absolutely upon his craft, he is doomed beyond hope.

So we of the *Deutschland* all knew what we owed to Chief Engineer Erbach, the constructor of our boat, and to the Germania Yard, where it was built. The *Deutschland's* quality is owing to Erbach's plans and the admirable co-operation of all the men who had her construction in charge.

All the work done upon the stocks at
Kiel in that amazingly short time during the winter of 1915, work exact and
minute to the most microscopic detail,
all that Herr Erbach had shown me
and taught me upon those unforgettable trial trips in the spring of the
same year—all these moral and material factors were now battling their
way across the storm-lashed ocean. We
were carrying a new glory of German
shipbuilding across the world.

To undergo a hurricane upon a U-
boat is quite another affair to encountering it upon a steamer—even of the
same tonnage. One must remain on
the surface as long as possible in order
to make progress with the powerful
oil engines. The electric power of the
storage batteries must be economized
for use in the most extreme emergen-

cies, as it would otherwise prove impossible to dive or manœuvre swiftly. But what is implied by a U-boat proceeding on the surface during a storm? It is always plunged up to the turret in water, and even the turret is covered by the waves. The seas go over the entire boat, since it is too heavy to be lifted like an ordinary craft and because, unlike a steamer, it cannot bring its "reserve displacement" to bear by boring into the oncoming seas. Its entire body is already submerged, and so it cannot possibly increase its displacement by plunging in still more deeply—thus attaining more buoyancy and momentum.

The elastic movements of the steamer, which continually changes its displacement during a heavy sea, and is lifted and supported by a constantly increasing impetus, is something that does not apply to the U-boat. Bellowing, and with fearful impact, the waves fall upon the trembling body of the ship. Its movements are direct and in jerks, and impose a tremendous strain upon all joints and ties.

It is ordeals such as these which test the material under a man's feet and show what genius went to the construction of a ship which is able to assert itself in the infernal cauldron of such a tempest, yet still make headway and obey the helm.

Yes, the *U-Deutschland* was put to a fearful test—and stood it wonderfully well. Matters looked ugly for several days. Tornado-like blasts whipped up the sea and flooded the vessel with thundering mountains of water. Naturally, all the manholes of

the deck were battened down. Even
that one which opened upon the platform of the turret and was so well
protected by the wall of the "bath-tub"
had to be banged shut at short intervals by the officer on watch—whenever
a sea came roaring up.

It was no joke—this duty upon the
turret. Still, it was infinitely more
desirable than to remain below decks
where the confined air and the ever-
lasting rolling and pitching of the vessel began to play havoc with the men,
who all suffered from sea-sickness.
Many an old experienced sailor made
his first offering to Neptune under
such conditions.

On the third day the weather at last
began to abate. The seas subsided and
we were able to open all the various
manholes so as to air the interior and

© Int. Film Service

Left—CAPTAIN HINSCH,
of North German Lloyd

Center—CAPTAIN PAUL KÖNIG

Right—PAUL G. L. HILKEN,
American Manager, German Ocean Navigation Co.

ASHORE AT BALTIMORE AFTER MANY DAYS AT SEA

First picture of the crew of the *Deutschland* taken on arrival

help it to dry. All the men of the watch off duty came up to stretch and sun themselves on the deck. Some of them needed it badly. They came up from below with pale faces and weary eyes. But no sooner did they snuff the fresh sea-breezes than they would light up their beloved weeds.

As few steamers were to be expected along our present route, we decided to have a great drying-out. Every man brought up his damp things — which would never dry in the confined air below—to be aired above deck. The whole deck was full of mattresses, blankets, clothes and boots. The underwear was fastened to the wires of the hand-rail and fluttered merrily in the wind as upon a wash-line. The men lay about between and sunned themselves like lizards. In order to increase the fan ventilation of the quarters below by good draughts of natural air, wind catchers were put up around all the manholes or trap-doors. These have scalloped side-wings and resemble the fins of fish. The curved, greenish body of the *Deutschland* rigged out with these things took on the appearance of some fantastic prehistoric fish-monster. We must have presented a remarkable spectacle!

But there was nobody about to see us or express surprise. A single steamer came popping up on the horizon toward evening, heralded by its smoke, but we were able to keep clear by a change of course.

The spirit of the men was splendid. One of the signs of this was the voice of the gramophone from the quarters of the crew. We also had our "canned music" in the officers' mess—for life aboard a U-boat would be unthinkable without it.

The more or less monotonous part of our voyage now began. The weather remained fair—we did not expect to meet with many craft.

I find the following note in my log-book:

"The boring part of our trip has now arrived. The boat keeps on her course always twisting a little, now and then we evade a steamer. Days go by without our seeing anything whatsoever. The gramophones play and everybody is in excellent spirits. A U-boat on the high seas makes a man more dependent upon the weather than any other spot in the world."

This was really the first opportunity we had had for breathing freely. We looked backward, we looked forward, and all of us grew more communicative under the influence of this eternal sameness of the sea.

I happened to be standing on the foredeck one day. Beside me, in the open wooden shell which covers the small, raised deck amidships beneath which our life-boat is stored, crouched our gigantic boatswain, Humke. Several fastenings had been loosened during the stormy days, and these had to be tightened. I had been standing there for quite a while, gazing westward, my thoughts fixed upon America —our goal.

I was suddenly moved by a strong desire to talk to that good soul Humke about these things. I asked him what he thought of our voyaging to America in the very midst of the war. What

was his opinion as to the purpose of
our enterprise?

The worthy fellow grinned and
replied at once: "Why, to make
money!"

This was a bit too summary for me,
and I tried to make him understand
what it would mean to resume our
trade relations with America—in the
very midst of war and in the face of
all the English blockading squadrons.
I also explained to him the purpose of
the British blockade. He answered
quickly in his Hamburg dialect: "Yes,
now I know just what these Englanders
are aiming for with their blockade."

I went further and explained to
him as best I could, the essentials and
the meaning of an effective blockade.
His answer was given with all the
naive assurance of our seamen and

with the real accent of the soul of the populace:

"*Ach!* they won't get *us*, anyway! And then, what's the use of that whole English blockade, eh?"

In the meantime, several men of the watch off duty had come up and were listening to my talk. There they stood, with legs far apart, on the deck of a small U-boat in the middle of the Atlantic—broad-shouldered, fearless German seamen.

"Well, now," I said, "you have now heard why we are pounding away across these seas. But I should like to say a little more to you.

"My dear fellows! It is hard to realize the real meaning of this trip of ours! Our gallant little *Deutschland* represents much more than a U-freight boat, with which we are carrying German goods to the Americans. These goods, of course, are such as English trade-envy and English craft have prevented from reaching America up to now. And this not only in order to damage German exports, but to draw profit from the disadvantages of others—to injure American manufacturers and American trade in a most serious fashion. Well, we'll do our little best to end that! But that is not all by any means. The appearance of the first trade submarine means much more. Without carrying a single gun or a torpedo, our good ship *Deutschland* will help to revolutionize the nature of all sea-traffic, not only as regards the entire trans-oceanic commerce, but also all international law—a revolution of the most far-reaching consequences.

"What has been the history of sea-traffic in this war—and of the U-boats of our Navy? We used these boats in order to protect ourselves against the barbaric methods of starvation so contrary to all international law. And what did the English then do? They armed their merchant-ships and bombarded every U-boat which approached them for the legal purpose of sinking contraband. And this is what these people call defense.

"What was the natural result of this? We protect ourselves and our submarines, toward which every fishing-trawler is apt to prove a *Baralong* butcher, and without warning we sink these armed English merchant-ships so that we ourselves may not be suddenly sunk by shell-fire or by ramming.

"And then the English begin to whine for help. And with international law as it at present stands, they manage to win the Americans to their point of view; for as the law at present exists, there are no regulations for submarines. We desire only peace with the great American people and so we give way. That government which rewarded the Captain of the *Baralong* appears to have carried off a victory—it has been decided that merchant vessels are not to be sunk without warning.

"And now our *Deutschland* comes along. It is a U-boat and a merchant vessel. Merchant vessels are not to be sunk without warning—the law as it exists contains no regulations for U-boats. But a merchant submarine which must be examined before it is

sunk would be rather difficult to capture—so long as it is capable of diving. Here the swiftest torpedo-boat is
quite powerless.

"The English have been caught in
their own trap. The *Deutschland*
brings about the collapse of this entire
one-sided interpretation of the formal
law. That which was first used against
us now becomes our defense.

"Things now stand thus: If merchant vessels, which, of course, may
also be built as submarines, must not
be sunk without examination, then our
Deutschland under the existing laws
has vitiated the right of the English
blockade. For I should like to see the
German merchant U-boat which an
English patrol steamer could approach
close enough to examine.

"Or, if the U-boat is not to be

searched, then merchant vessels may be sunk without warning—including the English. Thus the laws of warfare would once more be brought into a just equipoise by means of a peaceful, unarmed merchant-submarine.

"Such, my men, is the tremendous importance which devolves upon the appearance of our *Deutschland.*"

And thus I closed what I think was the longest speech which I ever made in my life.

The beautiful weather continued. The barometer remained at fair, the atmosphere dry and clear. We gradually approached the latitudes in which fair weather may be expected during this season of the year. The warmth of the sun's rays was making itself felt, and we began to plan ways of refreshing ourselves.

Our "surf-bath" was one of the best of these. This was the invention of our engine-watchman, Kissling. He usually had no interest in anything except his motors. For these he was animated by a most touching and unparalleled devotion. How often, when high seas were raging, had I seen a man pop up through the turret manhole and attempt to force himself in blind haste through the "bath-tub" without regard to the sublime acts of navigation which were just being performed there. And whenever the officer on watch was about to remonstrate angrily over this disturbance, it was always our valiant Kissling who, impelled by a deep anxiety for his motors, and garbed in his oldest oilskins, would go scrambling across the dripping and flooded decks toward the stern to have a look at his exhaust-pipes. He was also moved to examine the combustion of his motors a thousand times a day—to see if the pulse-beat of his engines was all it should be and the explosions regular. He was entirely absorbed by his beloved engines, and their rhythm became part of his life. He could sense the slightest irregularity in their working, and would not rest until he had found and removed it.

He must have been struck by the idea during one of his rather dangerous expeditions across the sloping, slippery decks. Anyway, he made us all happy one day with his invention of the "surf-bath." The thing was quite simple and obvious—like all great inventions.

In order to understand it properly, you must picture to yourself the outer superstructure of the *Deutschland*. The outer hull which gives its distinctive shape to the vessel is built over the cylinder-like compression hull and the lateral submersion tanks and oil-bunkers. The upper part of this outer hull also contains the so-called outer tanks, which are always flooded when the ship is loaded. Water and air have ingress to these tanks through many openings, holes and slits, that diving and rising may be facilitated. The outer tanks, therefore, play no part so far as the floating capacity of the vessel goes. They are a mere result of the outer skin which gives the craft its shiplike shape. Toward the top, this outer shell does not follow the shape of the compression hull and tanks. In spite of their comparatively minor importance, the outer tanks must naturally be accessible from above. This is made possible by large covers which are fitted into the outer shell. There are also ladders which facilitate descent into the tanks. When standing on the so-called tank-deck, there is still enough room between this and the deck line for a man to stand erect in the outer tanks.

When the ship is under way, the sea-water, of course, comes pouring into this large space from all sides. One need only step into the manhole after removing the covers in order to enjoy a most wonderful and absolutely safe ocean "surf-bath."

We made frequent use of this idea and had splendid baths.

There was only one disadvantage.

In case you stepped into the "surf-bath" after we had risen from a submersion you would be given not a surf but a regular oil-bath. The oil-bunkers are seldom hermetically tight, especially after a long and difficult course. And so it happens that the rising boat frequently breaks through a layer of its own oil as it mounts to the surface. This layer of oil then settles upon the "bath-tub," the covers of the manholes and the decks. In the outer tanks it naturally remains upon the surface of the water, which cannot change very rapidly here. It usually took more than a day before the stale, oily water had streamed away from these tanks and been replaced by new. So whoever happened to make use of the "surf-bath" during this period would come out but little

CAPTAIN PAUL KÖNIG
Photograph taken in Baltimore on arrival of
the *Deutschland*

PAUL G. L. HILKEN
American Manager German Ocean Navigation Co.

refreshed and with a skin that shone
in all colors, like that of the "Nickel-
man" in Hauptmann's "Sunken Bell."
The crew, of course, always took a
special delight in this metamorphosis.

The fine weather also gave an opportunity to play another sort of game
with my men—something that was not
without bearing upon the smooth progress of our voyage. We got out our
sextants and proceeded once more to
get our exact bearings by means of the
sun. We had been able to locate ourselves only approximately during the
stormy days that had preceded this fair
spell. The marvellously clear air impelled me to exercise myself at dusk
in the observation of stars and in
computing the height of the con-
stellations.

After my long period of idleness
ashore I felt a positive need to pro-
duce my chronometer and sextant and
to calculate a proper bearing under
these most remarkable circumstances.

Astronomical navigation aboard a
U-boat is not a particularly easy task.

An old steamer captain cannot but
feel a trifle queer when navigating a
craft of this sort through the great
trade routes—and a by no means tiny
craft—from the low post of vantage
of a turret. One does not have the customary outlook upon the sea; one has
to reckon with a factor of movement
that is quite strange; one must accus-
tom oneself to a new method of ma-
nœuvering and to new conditions of
command and the estimation of distance. But it is especially strange to
take the attitude of the sun from the

narrow "bath-tub" of a submarine
turret, or to check off a course or
reckon out a latitude. One is accustomed to carry out one's measurements
and reckonings at ease from the broad
bridge of a great liner—high above
the water—and to have all the necessary data promptly furnished by the
signalman. From the bridge one pro-
ceeds to the adjoining chart-room
whence, upon a large chart-table, one
can proceed to make one's calculations
in ease and comfort.

And now as to methods upon the
U-boat. Jammed in an oval steel tank
of about the size of a lady's small
trunk, you cling for dear life to a
small flap-seat, press one shoulder
against the parapet and try to hold the
sextant upright with a convulsive grip
—until the image of the sun appears

directly on the artificial horizon. You
are then obliged to shield the instrument quickly behind the protecting
wall and to scuttle down the ladder
into the central, just as you had pre-
viously scuttled up—hugging the in-
struments and charts against your
breast and bracing yourself with back
and knees. You then wedge yourself
once more through the turret manhole,
your eye kept peeled for every breaker,
and get to work with compass and
parallel ruler.

Your chart-table is your knee, and
you have the consciousness of having
made your entire calculations in a
cowering attitude.

What joy under such circumstances
to be able to work quietly on deck with
a smooth sea and a clear sky!

The experimental divings which we

made almost every day, were greatly facilitated by the fine weather. Everything chimed perfectly. We would be able to approach the American coast in peace and to dive into the three-mile limit.

During these experimental diving tests we were treated to a spectacle of fairy-like loveliness.

I had set the rudder in such a way that the turret was traveling about three yards under water. Overhead the sun shone brilliantly and filled the deeps with a clear radiance. The pure water was luminous with color—close at hand it was of a light azure blue, of fabulous clearness and transparent as glass. I could see the entire boat from the turret windows. The shimmering pearls of the air-bubbles which rise constantly from the body of

the craft played about the entire length
of the vessel from deck to bows, and
every detail stood out in miraculous
sharpness. Farther ahead there was a
multi-colored twilight. It seemed as if
the prow kept pushing itself noiselessly into a wall of opalescent green
which parted, glistening, and grew to
an ethereal, rainbow-like translucency
close at hand

We were spell-bound by this vision
of beauty. The fairy-like effect was
increased by medusæ which, poised in
the transparent blue, frequently became entangled in the wires of the
mine-guards or the railings and glowed
like trembling fires of rose, pale gold
and purple. We saw no fish at this
low depth. The following day we had
a little experience which provided
great fun for us, even though the end

was different from what we had expected.

My ambition had been aroused by the various successes which my comrades of the fleet and the merchant-marine had achieved by hiding the identity of their ships by means of paint or other disguises, so as to deceive the enemy.

During the fine weather we had prepared a most marvelous framework—representing the outline of a steamer. This would serve to hide our U-boat character to steamers passing at a considerable distance. A smoke-stack had been rigged up out of canvas and this could be fastened to the periscope by means of wire tackle and rings. It was able to rear proudly into the air.

A mask of canvas had been made for the disguising of the turret—this would give it the appearance of a small freight-boat.

Thus prepared for all emergencies, we boomed along in the most beautiful sunshine, when one evening, at half-past seven, a steamer suddenly loomed up to starboard. We soon realized that she would have to pass quite close to us should we keep on our course. We therefore edged off a little and proceeded to put our disguise to a test.

The "smoke-stack" was hoisted upon the periscope and the wind blew it out to an imposing size. In order to give it still more reality, we burned a handful of oil-soaked cotton waste at its lower end. The turret disappeared behind a somewhat fluttery "upper works."

But the undutiful cotton-waste consented merely to glow and refused to give out any smoke. Everybody stood round with puffed-up cheeks and blew and blew. Then the wireless operator, an inventive Berliner, fetched an air-pump and started a fearful fire in our imaginary furnaces. He was rewarded with a cheer, and above the edge of our "smoke-stack" appeared a thin little cloudlet which immediately dissolved into nothingness.

We laughed, and were about to proceed smokeless upon our way when Humke, the boatswain, appeared with a can full of tar. The air-pump once more performed its duty and at length the smoke-stack might literally have been described as vomiting smoke.

The effect was startling. For the steamer suddenly changed her course and—steered directly toward us!

This was not precisely what we had

worked for. I at once ordered our
mast to be dismounted and to clear
ship for diving. The canvas superstructure disappeared and the magnificent smoke-stack made a bow and col-
lapsed.

But the steamer had no sooner seen
this and recognized us as a U-boat
than she was seized with a blind con-
sternation. She once more veered
about and began to take to her heels,
pouring out thick clouds of smoke—
which we could not help regarding
with a certain amount of envy.

But undismayed we once more
hoisted our stack. The masts went up
again and while the steamer went
plunging off in desperate haste, we
stood and laughed until the tears rolled
down our cheeks. The humor of the
thing was simply overwhelming.

Our beautiful framework, which was intended to hide the character of our craft and render us inconspicuous, was precisely what had first attracted the attention of the gallant steamer. She apparently took us for a wreck or a ship in distress and came on with the best of intentions, only to be suddenly confronted with the diabolical subterfuge of a hypocritical submarine!

I wonder what the people aboard her thought after they had recovered from their first fright? I presume that they finally concluded to be monstrously proud of having escaped this latest trick of the "pirates" in such a skillful fashion.

We ourselves would have been far prouder had our framework performed its functions in better style.

We did not permit ourselves to be

discouraged, however, but improved our devices. We met with great success two days later, when we went bowling past a steamer—coming in the opposite direction—under a tremendous development of smoke and without being recognized.

VIII

HELL WITH THE LID ON

JUNE was drawing to a close and with it, unfortunately, the good weather.

A rising swell from the southwest, and the absence of the hoped-for favorable current, were signs that there was a storm-center progressing along the southern reaches of the Gulf Stream.

We proceeded thus for another day.

Toward evening it began to grow sultry and oppressive; the sun sank doubtfully behind blood-red veils of mist.

A wicked-looking sky and lively sheet lightning, as well as the rapidly increasing hot humidity of the atmosphere, proclaimed that we were in the neighborhood of the Gulf Stream. Toward night, tremendous thunderstorms came on, with a wind that came raging from all directions at once, and a wild, cross-running sea, which made steering very difficult.

We tested the temperature of the water. It mounted gradually to 28⁰ *Celsius.*

We were in the Gulf Stream, which defines its periphery in the airs above it with a fiery wreath of heavy tropical storms.

There was a strong phosphorescence of the sea and violent atmospheric disturbances—all of which are accompanying phenomena of the Gulf Stream. We were aware of this by the behavior of our wireless apparatus, which was irritated by the heavily charged electric atmosphere and began to go on strike. Until now the faithful thing had transmitted to us the German military bulletins of the station Nauen without interruption, day after day.

The phosphorescence of the sea seriously hindered the lookout. One was almost blinded, the eyes grew painful, and the vision became unsteady through this persistent coruscation of the waves in the coal-black night. This was rather uncomfortable, for we had now reached a region which was intersected by many steamer routes, and it was necessary to take double precautions.

In addition to this, the weather grew extremely vicious. A rough sea began to rise. Heavy showers of hail came rattling down upon the decks, and the waves were lashed into foam. The wind increased to velocity 11 to 12.

In the mighty vault above this seething ocean hung heavy, dun-colored masses of clouds which flung forth fallow lightnings without pause—whole broadsides of lightnings. Then the skies suddenly sank back into stygian night while the ship and the surrounding water went flaming up in greenish fire until every detail stood out in all its starkness.

The whole heavens were now converted into a bellowing chaos. One single and unbroken salvo of crashing thunder went rolling over us. We reached the very center. A maniacal witch's dance of primeval tempests raged around the boat. It seemed to be the end of all things. Then sud-

A CLOSE VIEW OF THE COMMANDING TOWER AND PERISCOPE OF THE "DEUTSCHLAND"

denly behind us the top-lights of a great liner came into view. We were able to avoid her course owing to the darkness. She passed by some distance away like a luminous apparition. Judging by her course, this passenger ship must have hailed from the Mediterranean. I must confess that we followed her rows of lights with some little feeling of envy until the rain and the darkness once more swallowed her up. The storm reached its height on the following day. Hurricane blasts came sweeping along and the air was filled with unceasing showers of spray. The water no longer came down in threads. These were cascades; these were walls of water which came plunging down upon us, whipping our faces and hands until they smarted with pain. The rain was so thick that one was no longer able to see. In order merely to see a yard or two, it was necessary to hold a small pane of glass in front of one's eyes—with the result that a small waterfall ran from the glass into one's sleeve.

The boat labored fearfully in this mad sea. The waves threw it back and forth, so that it creaked in every joint and rivet. Sometimes it heeled over to such an extent that one was scarce able to cling to the parapet of the "bath-tub."

It was an inferno, pure and simple.

But this was as nothing compared to the hell down below, especially in the engine-room.

This ferocious sea had naturally forced us to keep all openings battened down. Even the manhole in the turret could only be kept open at intervals. It is true that two large ventilation fans were going continuously, but the fresh air which they sucked down from the carefully protected ventilation shaft was at once devoured by the greedy Diesel motors. These hungry monsters out of sheer ingratitude, returned us nothing but heat—a heavy, oppressive heat, saturated with a frightful smell of oil, which the ventilating fans kept whipping and whirling through all the chambers of the boat. A refreshing effect could hardly be expected from ventilation such as this!

In addition to this, the air in the boat was saturated with moisture to an almost unbelievable degree. It no longer seemed possible to breathe and with a resigned hangman's humor we faced the moment which would convert us into fish. When the hatches are closed down, water is precipitated through all parts of the isolated body of the ship—a heavy sweat which the heat once more converts into vapor, until everything is soaked and grows mouldy. All the drawers and the doors of the cupboards swell and jam. Then there are the wet garments in which the watch descends from the turret, and these help to spread a pestilence through the narrow space.

You can have no conception of the atmosphere that is evolved by degrees under these circumstances, nor of the hellish temperature which brews within the shell of steel.

While in the Gulf Stream we had an outer temperature of 28° *Celsius.* This was about the warmth of the surrounding water. Fresh air no longer entered. In the engine-room two 6-cylinder combustion motors kept hammering away in a maddening two-four time. They hurled the power of their explosions into the whirling crank-shafts. The red-hot breath of the consumed gases went crashing out through the exhausts, but the glow of these incessant firings remained in the cylinders and communicated itself to the entire oil-dripping environment of steel. A choking cloud of heat and oily vapor streamed from the engines and spread itself like a leaden pressure through the entire ship.

During these days the temperature mounted to 53° Celsius.

And yet men lived and worked in a hell such as this! The watch off duty, naked to the skin, groaned and writhed in their bunks. It was no longer possible to think of sleep. And when one of the men fell into a dull stupor, then he would be aroused by the sweat which ran incessantly over his forehead and into his eyes, and would awake to new torment.

It was almost like a blessed deliverance when the eight hours of rest were over, and a new watch was called to the central or the engine-room.

But there the real martyrdom began. Clad only in an undershirt and drawers, the men stood at their posts, a cloth wound about their foreheads to keep the running sweat from streaming into their eyes. Their blood hammered and raced in their temples. Every vein boiled as with fever. It was only by the exertion of the most tremendous will-power that it was possible to force the dripping human body to perform its mechanical duty and to remain upright during the four hours of the watch. . . .

But how long would we be able to endure this?

I no longer kept a log during these days and I find merely this one note: "Temperature *must* not rise any higher if the men are to remain any longer in the engine-room."

But they *did* endure it. They remained erect like so many heroes, they did their duty, exhausted, glowing hot, and bathed in sweat, until the storm center lay behind us, until the weather cleared, until the sun broke through the clouds, and the diminishing seas permitted us once more to open the hatches.

And then these men came up out of

their hell; pale, streaming with oil and covered with grime, they came up to the light of day and rejoiced in the sunlight as though it shone for them for the first time.

IX

AMERICA

WHILE we had avoided all passing steamers upon the Atlantic, by adopting another course when the weather permitted, and even risked being seen once or twice, we now dived without exception as soon as we saw a cloud of smoke upon the horizon. Under no circumstances did we wish to reveal our presence as we made for the region of the coast, since we had to reckon with the possibility of encountering enemy warships.

On the 8th of July we began to notice by the color of the water that we could no longer be very distant from the goal of our voyage.

During the course of the afternoon, I consulted with my officers regarding the course toward Cape Henry, the southerly point of the two ranges of foothills which form the entrance to Hampton Roads and Chesapeake Bay.

I was of the opinion that we should wait in deep water for the coming of the dawn at a distance of about ten miles from the American three-mile limit, and then assure ourselves as to whether any hostile measures had been taken against us. In case indefinite rumors of our voyage had leaked out, there was small doubt but that we would have to reckon with such measures on the part of the enemy.

Krapohl, on the other hand, proposed that we approach the coast as closely as possible under cover of the night, and he was supported in this by Eyring.

Both plans had their pros and cons, and so I decided to proceed further toward the coast in the dusk and then to wait and see what the weather conditions would turn out to be.

The final decision was soon brought about by the coming up of a stiff southwest breeze. This gave us a good range of vision, which had not been the case with the summer weather that had hitherto prevailed. The breeze, however, also brought with it a violent rocking of our boat, which, with the short and choppy sea that now developed, became extremely disagreeable. We therefore decided, without further hesitation and upon the basis of exact astronomical calculations made a short time before, to steer at night for the shore lights of Cape Henry and Cape Charles.

We proceeded at once on our way. After some time, a pale glow became perceptible upon the horizon. It came up spasmodically and then vanished again. This was the glow of the revolving light upon Cape Henry.

It was the first greeting from America.

Suddenly, upon our starboard bow, a white light flashed up. It disappeared instantly and then flickered up again several times. Immediately afterward another white light appeared off our port bow, and this remained fixed.

We looked at one another.

What the devil did this mean? It looked confoundedly as though war vessels with blinded lights were making light signals to each other.

At all events, we must keep an infernally sharp lookout.

With engines going at half-speed, and submerged up to the turret, with all men at their diving-posts, we crept closer, keeping the sharpest lookout, and drilling into the darkness with our glasses.

It was not long before we saw that the fixed light belonged to the top lantern of a harmless outcoming steamer, which passed us at a considerable distance off-stern. Soon after this, where the flickering light had been, we saw the outlined sails of a three-masted schooner. As is the custom with many of these coasting vessels, she was sailing without side-lights and merely displayed a white stern light from time to time. It was these lights which we had mistaken for the signalling of warships.

Considerably relieved, I ordered the engines full speed ahead. The reflex of the fixed light upon Cape Henry now came into view, while the intermittent blinking of Cape Charles grew brighter and brighter along the horizon.

We now knew that we had set our course correctly. The entrance between the two ranges of hills lay in front of us.

Soon the beacon lights themselves came up above the horizon. An indescribable feeling possessed my heart. I saluted Cape Charles' flashing fire, its tireless blades of light were a silent, but unmistakable symbol of security amidst the dark infinity that surrounded us. There, after our long and dangerous voyage, lay the land at last —our goal—America.

We now began to pass the bobbing lantern-buoys of the channel. I recognized the well-known howling of a whistling buoy with which I was familiar from my former trips, and so the sense of hearing also contributed to the feeling that land was close at hand.

After we had passed the whistling buoy we emerged completely. We now saw the lights of various passenger steamers. The steamers, however, did not observe us, as we still proceeded with blinded lights until we ran close off Cape Henry and had reached the American three-mile limit.

This was on the 8th of July, at half-past eleven at night.

Once within the American neutrality zone, we set our lights, and made our way quietly into the entrance between the two capes until we made out the red and white top-lights of the pilot steamer.

We stopped and burnt the customary blue fire. Hereupon the pilot boat at once directed its searchlight upon us, and as it was unable to see the outlines of a steamer, it approached us very carefully.

Again and again the long luminous arm of the searchlight kept feeling the low deck and the turret of the *Deutschland*.

The unexpected appearance of our boat seemed to have startled the good pilot to such an extent that it took him a long time to fire his question at us through the megaphone.

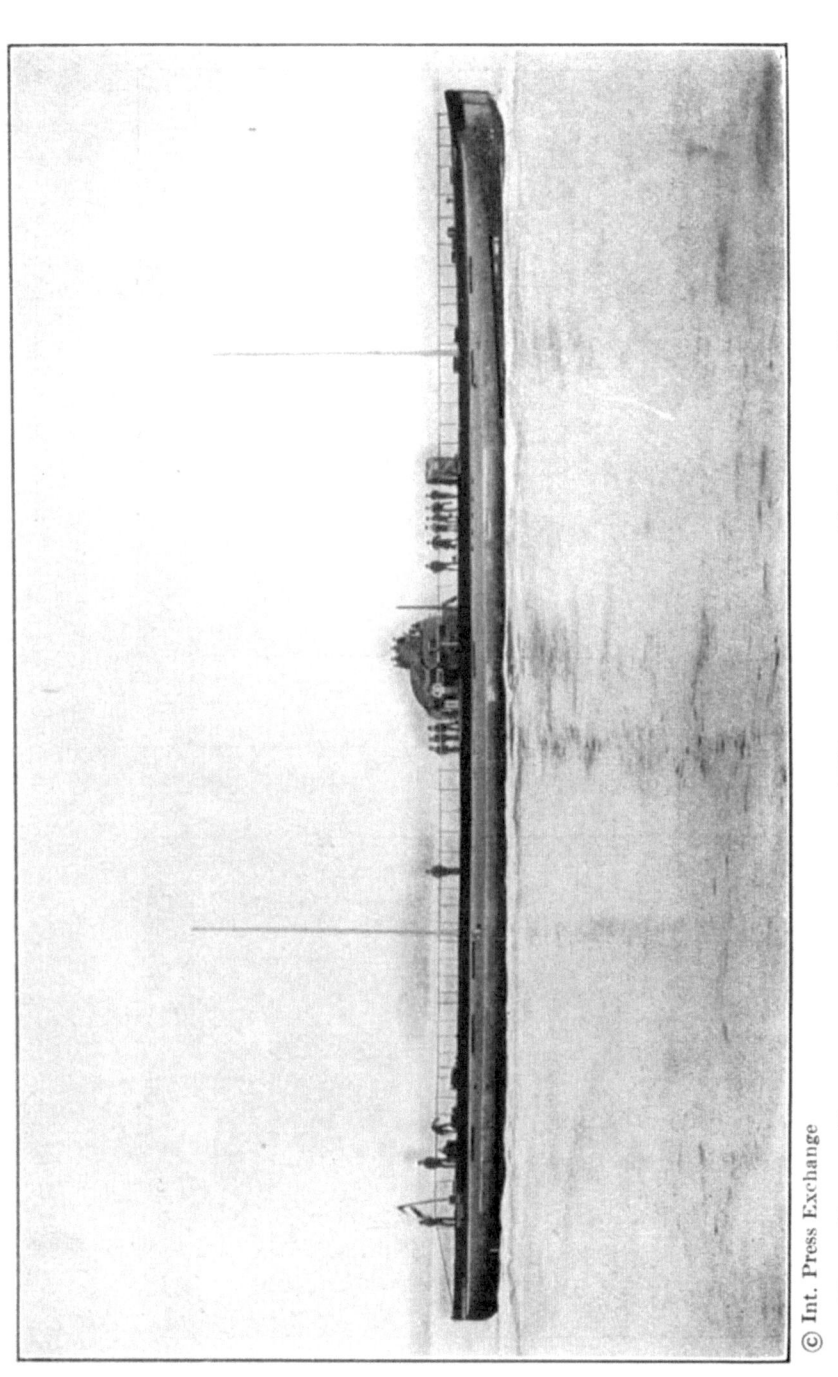

THE LAST PHOTOGRAPH OF THE "DEUTSCHLAND" LEAVING BALTIMORE AND
PASSING OUT TO SEA FROM CHESAPEAKE BAY

THE CREATORS OF THE SUBMARINE MERCANTILE SERVICE

DIRECTOR ZETZMANN
Builder of the Merchant Submarine
Deutschland

ALFRED LOHMANN
Founder of the German Ocean
Navigation Co.

"Where are you bound for?"

"Newport News," we replied.

He then inquired after the name of our ship, which we gave. But we were forced to repeat it twice before the men on the pilot boat were able to comprehend what an unusual visitor lay before them. There must have been something of a sensation aboard that pilot-boat.

A boat was quickly lowered, and as the pilot climbed over the round belly of the *Deutschland* up to our deck, he greeted us with these words, which must have come from the very depths of his heart:

"I'll be damned, here she is!"

Then he shook our hands again and again out of sheer honest heartiness, and gave vent to his genuine delight in being the first American to greet the *U-Deutschland,* in the land of liberty.

I at once asked our friend if he had heard anything of our being expected. Great was my joy and surprise when I learned that a tug-boat had been lying between the capes for the past few days, evidently looking for us.

We at once got under way with our good pilot in order to look for this tug-boat.

In the meantime, the incoming passenger steamers had also discovered the remarkable stranger. They lighted us up from all sides with their searchlights. And thus our arrival in American waters resolved itself into a fantastic nocturne.

The search for our tug-boat was, however, by no means easy in the darkness. We were obliged to search for a long time and finally discovered the craft after two hours.

She was the tow-boat *Timmins,* under command of Captain Hinsch, of the North German Lloyd.

And now great was our joy.

That valiant soul, Captain Hinsch, whose liner, the *Neckar,* has been lying in Baltimore since the outbreak of war, had waited for us more than ten days between the two capes.

Our long absence had already caused him the greatest anxiety as to our fate.

He was now unutterably happy to see his long-awaited *protégé* safe and sound before him. He then communicated to us the order that we were to proceed to Baltimore instead of Newport News. Here everything had been prepared for our arrival.

We now took farewell of our cheery

Newport News pilot, and made our way up Chesapeake Bay, accompanied by the *Timmins.* We proudly hoisted the German flag, which no doubt fluttered for the first time in these waters since the *Eitel Friedrich* ran into Hampton Roads.

Thus in the gray of the morning, we entered the Bay. Our course gradually became a triumphal procession. All the neutral steamers that we passed, American and others, saluted us with three blasts of their sirens and steam whistles. Only an English steamer swept by us in a poisonous silence, the while we let the black-white-red banner stream proudly in the wind. Captain Hinsch upon his tug-boat kept an eagle eye upon the Englishman, lest he should chance to slip his rudder a bit and ram us by mere accident.

The gallant *Timmins* was helpful to us in other ways. We were able to answer the greetings of the steamers only by means of our siren, which was operated with our precious compressed air. This would in the end, have become a rather expensive pleasure, and so the *Timmins* undertook the duty of making our responses with her big steam whistle.

The farther we moved up the bay, the madder grew the noise. We were delighted beyond measure with this, for we could plainly perceive in this uproar the sympathies which the Americans cherished for us and our voyage.

About four o'clock in the afternoon, the *Timmins* carefully came alongside. A block of ice was handed over to us, a couple of bottles of champagne were rapidly cooled, and we proudly clinked our glasses to the safe arrival of the *Deutschland* in America. We merely regretted that it was only the corks which popped over to Captain Hinsch.

What this first iced drink meant to us can only be appreciated by him who is able to picture to himself what it means to have lived day after day in a temperature of 53° *Celsius*.

The rumors of our arrival must have spread with miraculous rapidity, for to our great astonishment boats full of reporters and film operators began to meet us while we were still many miles from Baltimore.

Although it was already growing dusk, we were nevertheless subjected to a violent bombardment by the cameras. We should also most likely have had to undergo an endless series of questions and calls had not the weather-god of Chesapeake Bay, casting a hospitable eye upon our need of rest, come to our assistance. A heavy thunderstorm now broke and in place of a flood of questions, we scorched and tanned navigators were refreshed by a cooling flood of rain. The *Deutschland,* accompanied by the trusty *Timmins,* once more pursued her way, lonely and silent, through the falling night toward her final goal.

At eleven o'clock at night we stopped at the Baltimore Quarantine Station, and our anchor rattled for the first time into American waters.

U-Deutschland had arrived.

X

BALTIMORE

THE first thing upon which our eyes fell on the following morning was the stout and stubby tug-boat *Timmins,* which had made fast alongside us. There lay the faithful vessel keeping watch over us.

Soon after, about five o'clock, the physician of the Quarantine Station arrived. I at once handed to him the certificate of health which had been made out for us in due form on June 13th, by Mr. William Thomas Fee, the American Consul at Bremen. Then the doctor overhauled the boat and passed us after he had mustered the crew. Then, as the first American official to greet us, he called for three cheers for the *Deutschland* and her crew.

Then we weighed anchor, and under the guidance of the *Timmins,* we proceeded to our anchorage at Locust Point, where we were to discharge our cargo.

No boat could have made her way more safely than we under the protection of the *Timmins* and the swarm of craft which had been hired by the film companies and now surrounded us. Five to six fellows stood, with cameras cocked, upon every one of these boats and did their best by means of cheery calls to induce us to assume more effective poses—such as are suitable for the heroes of the "movies."

"Show your face, Cap!"

"Turn your head!"

"Wave your hand!" And other such cries echoed from all sides, and these enterprising chaps turned the cranks of their machines like mad.

I stood on the turret and looked toward the left, and then I looked toward the right, and then I waved one hand and then the other. A request to smile was scarcely necessary, for the actions of the "movie" men were uncommonly funny.

And so we reached our anchorage at Locust Point in the best possible spirits.

Here everything had been prepared by Captain Hinsch through weeks of careful work. The *Deutschland* found the snuggest and safest kind of a berth here. It was so thoroughly protected from all outside approach by means of nets and beams that the boat seemed safe from all harm through human agency.

We lay alongside a wooden pier which was built out into the stream, and under cover of a large shed, in which the goods we were to carry back already lay stored. This region was so little frequented that communication between the pier and the nearest good street had first to be established.

The entire place toward the land side was cut off by a large ditch and barbed wire entanglements.

In the river the *Deutschland* was protected on one side by the pier and the North German Lloyd steamer *Neckar*. The *Neckar* had lain in Baltimore since the outbreak of war. It was now to serve as our home. From here we could always keep an eye on the *Deutschland*.

On the other side, the *Deutschland* was surrounded by an entire system of heavy beams, with strong nets, which reached to the bottom, so that it would have been impossible for even a diver to approach the vessel. In addition to this, there were several boats which mounted guard day and night, among them the *Timmins,* which would keep her tireless little searchlight playing over the entire vicinity all night long.

Nevertheless, there were several delightful little interludes. In order that the discharging and loading of the cargo might go on unobserved, a high fence had been built all around the shed. This rendered it impossible to see anything of the ship or the freight pier.

The only opportunity for having a look at the wonder-boat, and that at a

considerable distance, was offered by
a pile-driver which lay anchored in the
stream. This was soon utilized by the
newspaper reporters as a post of observation. Here they began to make their
perch, never taking their eyes from
us. They did regular sentry duty.
Two men were always crouched on top
of the swaying framework by day and
by night, in the self-sacrificial exercise of their profession.

We, too, established our sentries. At
night, when the watch was changed
upon the pile-driver across the way,
the searchlight operator aboard the
Timmins would amuse himself by flashing his light in that direction, courte-
ously escorting these gentlemen upon
their risky climb. As they clambered
down from the framework, the rays
would follow and outline them, one

after the other, like spiders under a pocket flash-lamp.

Captain Hinsch had simply provided for everything, from our reception and safe conduct to our housing and provisioning upon the *Neckar.*

The only means of access to the *Deutschland* was by way of this steamer—at least for those few privileged people who were permitted to view the vessel—if only from without. Otherwise, all visits to the boat were strictly forbidden. Of course, we should have been quite happy to show off this child of our pride to all comers, but, in view of the danger of sabotage which might accrue to the first German submarine freight boat from an indiscriminate public inspection, we were forced on principle to adhere to our refusals, and so hundreds of Amer-

UP THE WESER TO BREMEN

icans, who had come in automobiles, sometimes from great distances, even from Western states, in order to have a look at the *Deutschland,* were forced, to our own deep regret, to go their ways without achieving their purpose.

The film companies, however, were able to score a triumph. I fulfilled their desire to immortalize the entire crew upon their first treading American soil. And so I permitted myself and my men to be taken outside in a proud group.

My first trip to the city resembled a triumphal procession. The auto was obliged to halt every moment, and I was congratulated upon all sides, and everybody wished to shake my hand. I grew to be a sort of obstruction to traffic during those first days in Baltimore.

Thus I slowly made my way to the
agency of the North German Lloyd.
This was surrounded by dense masses
of people.

It was first necessary to make the
usual declaration. I went to the Custom House authorities and made the
necessary visits. I was greeted everywhere in the heartiest manner.

Then I went back to the Agency, and
summoned up my entire stock of seaman's resolutions in order to devote myself to the press. I took up my position behind a barrier, that is to say,
behind the counter of the Passenger
Office before which an enormous crowd
was pushing. I was quite alone, and
held my defences against hundreds—
men and women, each of whom wanted
to know something different, each of
whom asked me questions, from the

most insignificant personalities to questions of higher politics.

One lady cried: "Do, Captain, tell me, what is it like in a submarine? . . . ." Another asked, full of sympathy: "Say, is it true that in Germany the babies are starving for want of milk?" A prosperous looking man proclaimed his interest in the problems of diet by demanding: "Say, Captain, what did you live on?"

I was also frequently asked: "What about the Kaiser's message you brought over for Mr. Wilson?" I was as little able to reply to this question as to that other, so frequently put: "When do you expect to leave Baltimore again?"

And I was supposed to answer hundreds of similar questions with my one poor little voice. I stood there like a breakwater and the floods went surg-

ing about me, mounting higher and
higher, until my whole spiritual ego
was swallowed up, only to re-appear
the next day in fragments scattered
throughout the press of two hemi-
spheres.

My body, however, somewhat wearily
obeyed an invitation of the German
club where our arrival was celebrated
in exclusive German circles, and where
we spoke with love and pride of the
battling Fatherland.

———

The following days were to become
one continual festival for us. Only
those who know American hospitality
and American enthusiasm can form an
idea of the hearty reception we were
given everywhere. People's heads were
quite turned. It did **one good** to see

with how much open and honest sympathy our voyage and safe arrival were regarded by the Americans, and how this sympathy was expressed with the most unrestrained rapture.

Wherever we went, we were greeted in the most fervent fashion. Our hands were shaken. The "Wacht am Rhein" was sung and wildly enthusiastic ovations were given us everywhere. It simply snowed invitations upon the officers and crew. Festivals and parties were arranged for us, and on one occasion, when two of my officers of the watch, accompanied by a friend, were recognized in a large public resort, the concert music suddenly stopped, the limelight was thrown upon these gentlemen, and amidst tremendous jubilation the band played "America" and the "Wacht am Rhein."

While the people of the United States, of all classes and conditions, were thus recording their unrestrained admiration for the *Deutschland,* the American Government had also taken up an official position in regard to the question whether our boat was to be considered a merchant vessel or whether, as expressed in the emphatic protest of the British and French Ambassadors, it was to be considered in the nature of a war vessel.

A Government Commission of three American naval officers came down from Washington on July 12th. They were to make a most detailed inspection of the *Deutschland.* Since we had absolutely no armament of any nature, and no provisions for mounting any on board, we were able to show these gentlemen everything with absolute confidence.

After an examination of three hours, which covered every nook and corner of the boat, and which cost the participants much perspiration in crawling about the hot and glowing steel hull, the Commission confirmed the purely mercantile character of the *U-Deutschland*. These gentlemen were full of intense admiration for the genius shown in the construction of the entire boat, and were particularly impressed by the staggering fact of the complicated nature of the entire mechanism.

The numerous German-Americans in Baltimore organized a German Festival in honor of the entire crew and for the benefit of the Red Cross. This event took place in Cannstädter Park,

a large popular resort near Baltimore.
There were rifle-ranges, booths for
raffles, an open-air stage, a dancing
pavilion and similar amusements in the
open. I must say that our men showed
off well at these affairs. They stood
the homage which was given them in
good style and displayed little shyness.
When it came to dancing, they swung
a leg with the best of them. I saw a
couple of my fine fellows dancing with
the ladies of our host's family as
though they had done nothing else all
their lives.

The whole constituted for us legendary seafarers one single, solid ovation of overpowering kindliness. Hundreds surrounded us and toasted
us again and again, and clamored
for a word with each and every one
of us.

Of course, I was especially singled out for these attentions. I was supposed to shake the hand of all the participants at this festival—this finally developed into a universally expressed desire.

The problem was not an easy one to solve. With considerable embarrassment, I looked around me and saw the countless hands which were stretched toward me, and gazed upon the faces of that vast crowd of gay and excited people who seethed about me.

At last the following plan was devised. I was put into a Committee automobile and the crowd was made to defile before me between Masters of Ceremony in the shape of policemen. I was thus able to shake the hand of everyone who went by. This procession lasted over an hour and a half, during which time I shook hands without pausing.

I marvel that my two hands are still attached to my arms.

On July 20th, the *Deutschland* received a visit from Count Bernstorff, the German Ambassador, who had come to Baltimore with several gentlemen from the summer seat of the Embassy. We showed them our faithful boat, whose inspection amidst the process of loading the cargo and in a terrific heat was scarcely an unalloyed pleasure.

On the evening of the same day, an official dinner was given by the Mayor of Baltimore in honor of the presence of the German Ambassador. This had been preceded by a small lunch in the select precincts of the Germania clubhouse. The dinner given by the Mayor, a most charming gentleman, was of an exclusively political nature, and was attended only by politicians and official personages. There was a long series of excellent courses and of drinks, and, according to American custom, the close of the dinner and the appearance of innumerable new drinks were the occasion for a number of speeches. In these the arrival of the *Deutschland* in America, the significance of this event to the city of Baltimore and for friendly German-American relations were duly celebrated.

Then the city band came into the garden and played the "Wacht am Rhein" and the American National Hymn, while the crossed American and German flags were unfolded.

This was a very pretty symbol of friendship and understanding between the two peoples, both of whose interests are bound up in the freedom of the seas.

While all these festivities were under way, and all our evenings thus employed, our cargo had been discharged and the stowing away of the new cargo had begun.

This is quite a chapter by itself.

Messrs. Paul G. L. and H. G. Hilken, two gentlemen who represent the North German Lloyd in Baltimore, had done their very utmost to lighten this most delicate part of our task and insure its success.

They had not only provided in all secrecy the necessary goods which were to constitute our return cargo, but they had already had these stored in the sheds ready for loading. It was a most impressive-looking pile and, on viewing it, one might well have doubted whether it would be possible to stow it all within the limits of one U-boat. Our friends had also seen to it that the special stevedores were at hand.

The entire work upon the boat and on the freight pier was carried out by negroes, whose slight degree of education and weak powers of observation were in this case a special recommendation. In addition to this, the negroes were thoroughly searched every time before beginning work, being forced to strip—all this in order to protect the boat from any premeditated outrage.

The discharging of the cargo was completed without any difficulty.

For those who are accustomed to the unloading of cargoes, a singular picture presented itself. Usually there are great derricks, steel windlasses and hydraulic cranes, and the heavy goods and cases are hoisted up out of the dark ship's hold amidst hubbub, thumpings and hissings. Stevedores and foremen stand beside yawning openings and shout in an inarticulate speech. Here, on the other hand, there were two small wooden hoists erected above the ordinary hatches of the U-boat, and these, with their neat little electric windlasses, did swift work. The goods came rushing up into the daylight in little sacks and chests, rapidly and noiselessly, almost as in a doll's theater. There was something miniature in the unloading of the U-boat in this manner.

It was really astonishing to observe the quantity of goods that piled themselves up on the pier, all of which had been fetched up out of the insignificant-looking whale-back through the narrow hatches.

The loading of the vessel was much more difficult. Special calculations had to be made for this by our submarine expert and "Master of U-boat cargoes," ship-architect Pruss of the Germania Yards. Every kilogram or pound of the cargo, differing so greatly in weight and bulk, had to be stowed away in some carefully calculated position, so as not to influence unfavorably the trimming of the vessel.

Careful storage was, moreover, of the utmost importance as the space available is, after all, more or less limited, and every case and every sack must be firmly fixed in position. Otherwise it might happen that the most disagreeable surprises would befall us during a storm, a sudden dive with a strong list, or other incidents. These might, by hindering our ability to manœuvre, lead to disaster.

A loading of this kind is therefore a very tedious one. The entire freight, sacks and boxes, must be passed into the narrow hatches by the negroes, after being weighed. Piece by piece the goods are placed upon the scales, the weights noted by the tally-meter and then called out and checked up in special lists.

These lists or tables were all studied out according to a theoretical plan. The efficiency of this plan was then tested by a trial dive and trimming test. There was just enough depth at our anchorage for us to carry this out.

For this trial dive all the men were

ordered to their stations. The submersion tanks were slowly opened and
the boat was filled with just enough
water to cause it to float with the
hatch of the turret appearing above
the surface.

In this position, the body of the
boat was made to oscillate by ballast-
ing the two trimming-tanks in different
ways. This permitted us to judge
whether the burdens in the boat had
been properly distributed. In case
there had been any shifting of the
weights, the cargo must have been
stowed anew. A final dive and trimming test was then necessary in order
to see that the lading of the boat was
correct in every detail.

Those two thousand tons in their
swaying and fluid element were brought
to a most delicate and absolute balance.

XI

FAREWELL TO BALTIMORE

I SHOULD like to set a motto above this description of our return trip. The words are taken from the London *Morning Post* of July 18th, and refer to the attitude assumed by the British Government with regard to the *Deutschland*.

"The *Deutschland*, in consequence of its character as a submarine, is to be regarded as a war vessel and is to be treated as such. The warships of the Allies will, therefore, seek every opportunity to waylay the vessel beyond the American three-mile limit and will sink it without warning."

[160]

Thus ran a cable dispatch which reached America from London on July 19th. And such were the words which we read for ourselves in a copy of the *Morning Post* which was sent to us toward the end of July.

This at least had the advantage of letting us know precisely what we had to expect.

Never had the English point of view, in all its brutality, been more clearly displayed.

We had no torpedo-tubes and no cannons on board. We had not the slightest possible means of making an attack. We did not even carry arms with which to defend ourselves, something which is permitted to every English merchant vessel; moreover, the biggest of the neutral powers had expressly recognized us as a merchant vessel, and yet we were to be sunk without warning!

We knew, therefore, what lay before us.

It had also become known that eight enemy war vessels with lookout boats and nets had assembled in front of Chesapeake Bay in order to capture us as soon as we left the American three-mile limit and to shatter us to pieces with mines like some blind fish.

Caution was, therefore, imperative—we should have to worm our way through with true U-boat craftiness.

But we also knew how to get the best of these English and French efforts as we had done once before. The penetration of the English blockade outward-bound from Europe had not been precisely a walk-over.

Nothing had tickled us more than to read the brilliant explanation which had been launched by Captain Gaunt of the British General Consulate in New York, when the first rumors of the voyage of a German U-boat to America had cropped up. Captain Gaunt is the naval expert at the Consulate, and the good man ought to know. He pacified the English public as follows: "It is impossible to send a submarine to America. Should the Germans, nevertheless, venture to try it we should seize it. A large submarine leaves a trail of oil and machine-grease on the water behind it. This trail can be followed by our swift cruisers and it is a dead certainty that they will capture the submarine."

We had, therefore, merely to see to it that our "capture" this second time

would prove to be this "dead certainty."

The first of August had arrived. We
had taken hearty farewells of everyone. All the formalities with the authorities had been settled and we were
free to put out to sea to keep our dates
with the gentlemen that prowled about
the entrance of the Bay.

Our departure was delayed, as we
had to wait for high water in order to
make our way out of the Patapsco
River, upon which Baltimore is situated, over the intervening mud-bank
into Chesapeake Bay. The tide rose
very slowly on this day, as there was
a north wind blowing, which was inclined to keep the stream from reaching Baltimore up the long, narrow
Bay.

We anxiously awaited the rising of

the water, and at last, at 3:20 in the afternoon, the moment had arrived. The lines were cast off—slowly the enclosing sentinel vessels opened out and majestically the *Deutschland* pushed her way from the pier into the channel. The tug *Timmins* steamed along beside us like a faithful shepherd-dog and seemed to growl whenever the numerous small and large boats loaded with reporters and film operators approached too closely.

There was nothing to fear. The boat of the Baltimore harbor-police had been kindly assigned to accompany us, and a Maryland revenue cutter had received orders to escort us to the limits of its territory.

Hundreds of people stood upon the banks of the Patapsco River. They waved to us and saluted our departure with constant cheers. All the tugs in the harbor set up a howling with their sirens and their whistles; the steamers dipped their flags and hooted; it was an appalling hubbub. But we knew, as we went on and outward, that innumerable hearts throughout this vast America accompanied us with their blessings and were waiting anxiously for the moment which would bring to them the certainty of our successful escape.

As soon as we reached the open waterway and set the engines going at full speed, our escorts gradually dropped behind; even the *Timmins* had all it could do to keep up. We remarked the slow speed of the American boats; the cheers grew weaker and weaker, the boats fewer and fewer, and finally only the revenue cutter remained. After this craft had vanished, about seven o'clock, we should have been alone with the *Timmins* had there not been another mysterious escort which could not so easily be shaken off.

This was a swift gray boat with a pointed snout and a flat, short stern, a sort of overgrown racing boat, of which it was rumored that it held some eighty horse-power in its belly, and could set up a pace of 22 miles. It was supposed to have been hired some ten days before by a certain gentleman, who paid the round sum of $200 per day, from which it was to be seen how highly this gentleman estimated the possibility of announcing his purely sporting interest by a match between his racer and the *Deutschland*.

In consciousness of its superior

speed, the pretty boat went pirouetting all around us. It described most admirable circles and curves; it cut caprioles, it buzzed about us like a blue-bottle and its high spirits were really alarming. The good old *Timmins* might growl as threateningly as you please with its steam siren and fling out angry clouds of smoke, but the eighty horse-power hummer hung on and would not be driven off.

We proceeded thus until nightfall.

Then, about eight o'clock, a slight breeze began to blow and it was not long before a low swell came up—a merry swell, which splashed gaily against the bows of the *Deutschland.*

Our blue-bottle friend had, in the meantime, hung out his lights, quite according to regulations, and we heard the water splashing about *his* bows as well. But he no longer raced about us, but went spattering along in our wake. It was a pretty sight to see his colored lights dancing behind us, or disappearing and reappearing amid the illuminated foam and the spray—growing ever more distant.

At ten o'clock there was a pretty neat little sea under way. The lights had dwindled to little points far astern, and as the gray dawn came up, the sea was clear; our little friend had evidently flown back home.

However, a great number of fishing-trawlers soon came looming up out of the gray murk so that we were somewhat fearful of running into a regular trap—even here amidst these neutral waters.

But loud hurrahs and waving of hands from these vessels soon enlightened us. It was a company of American press representatives who had not hesitated to make this nightly trip, together with a number of admirers and friends of the *Deutschland*, in order to offer final greetings to our boat some fifty miles out from Baltimore.

One steamer after another glided past us, and by six o'clock in the morning we were travelling in such free water that we were able to make our first diving-trial. After our long spell ashore, I wished to get the crew and the boat once more well in hand— merely on account of that "dead certain" capture.

So we underwent our first diving trial and everything went without a hitch. The *Timmins* remained in the neighborhood. Captain Hinsch told

me later that it was a startling sight
to see the *Deutschland* sink away so
silently, only to come pushing out of
the water a few moments later with a
foaming wave across her bows.

So the dive was a success. In order
to see that everything else was tight
and in good order, I gave the command to set the boat upon the sea
bottom at a spot which, according to
the reading upon the chart, had a
depth of some 30 meters.

Once again everything grew silent.
The daylight vanished, the well-known
singing and boiling noise of the submerging vents vibrated about us. In
my turret I fixed my eyes upon the
manometer. Twenty meters were re-
corded, then 25. The water ballast
was diminished—30 meters appeared
and I waited the slight bump which

was to announce the arrival of the boat at the bottom. . . .

Nothing of the sort happened.

Instead of this the indicator upon the dial pointed to 32—to 33—to 35 meters. . . .

I knocked against the glass with my finger—correct—the arrow was just pointing toward 36.

"Great thunder! what's up?" I cried, and reached for the chart. Everything tallied. Thirty meters were indicated at this spot and our reckoning had been most exact. . . .

And we continued to sink deeper and deeper.

The dial was now announcing 40 meters.

This was a bit too much for me. I called down to the central and got back the comforting answer that the large manometer was also indicating a depth of over 40 meters!

The two manometers agreed.

This, however, did not prevent the boat from continuing to sink.

The men in the central began to look at one another. . . .

Ugh! it gives one a creepy feeling to go slipping away into the unknown amidst this infernal singing silence and to see nothing but the climbing down of the confounded indicator upon the white-faced dial. . . .

There was nothing else to be seen in my turret. I glanced at the chart and then at the manometer in a pretty helpless fashion.

In the meantime the boat sank deeper; 45 meters were passed—the pointer indicated 48 meters. I began to think the depth of the Chesapeake

Bay *must* have some limit; we surely could not be heading for the bottomless pit? Then—the boat halted at a depth of 50 meters without the slightest shock.

I climbed down into the central and took counsel with Klees and the two officers of the watch.

There could be only one explanation; we must have sunk into a hole which had not been marked upon the chart.

Well, that did not matter much after all. It was a matter of indifference to us whether we ascended from a depth of 30 meters or one of 50.

I was just about to give the command to rise, when my eye fell upon the box compass which, with its delicate tremblings of the black and white dial, had always been accustomed to hang so cheerily in its little illuminated house. . ⟨•⟩ ⟨•⟩

I started back. . . . *Donnerwetter!* What did this mean?

The dial of the compass had become insane and was turning itself like mad upon its own axis without pause! . . .

Things were beginning to look uncomfortable.

As our box-compass was about the most reliable thing you could have found in all the world, and as the bottom of the Chesapeake Bay at a depth of 50 meters could not possibly have begun to rotate about us, there was only one conclusion to be arrived at— a most disquieting conclusion. . . .

We were cheerfully turning about in a circle in this hole of ours—and only the devil knew why.

I at once ordered the exhaust pumps

to begin their work. They took up their purring song, it is true—but in a lighter key and with an empty note. The pumps had no effect. We continued to stick in the mud—we did not move an inch.

This seemed to be the last straw, and I must say none of us was any too cheerful about the matter.

In the meantime we had sunk still deeper—according to the manometer. But now the revolving motion ceased and we lay perfectly quiet.

I once more gave the command—most energetically—to rise at once.

The pumps began to purr again, but once more they ran empty.

So *that* was no good.

We should have to proceed with quiet deliberation, otherwise we should still be in the same spot to-morrow.

THE TRIUMPHANT RETURN TO GERMANY

The *Deutschland* entering the mouth of the Weser

HOME AT LAST. THE "DEUTSCHLAND" ALONGSIDE ITS PIER IN BREMEN

After a good deal of working about, Engineer Klees finally succeeded in making the pumps act.

They began to force the water out of the tanks with a deep, hoarse note. They were working! Our eyes were fixed as if fascinated upon the index of the manometer. Hurrah! We were getting free, we were mounting. The indicator pointed to 49 meters. . . . Then once more I thought I could hardly believe my eyes. What the devil was up now? . . . The manometer suddenly announced 20 meters, then it went back to 49—then once more sprang up to 20—and so on and so on.

Things now began to be really critical. We stared at one another and were at our wits' end. We no longer knew what was the matter with the boat and everything else—we no longer knew at what depth we were lying. Even the manometer had now gone crazy!

In order fully to comprehend what this meant, you must remember that the men in a submerged submarine know nothing and see nothing except what the pointer of the manometer tells them. This is the only thing they can depend upon. When this ceases to function properly, you can only grope about in uncertainty.

Although our situation had become highly precarious, a stony calm prevailed in the boat. We were aware that in case the worst happened, we could still have recourse to the compressed air, which would have flung us toward the surface, even though the pumps did not work.

But this measure was not necessary. Klees had been thinking deeply. Then he darted for a lever. There was a rush and a roar of compressed air. The manometer made a wild kick toward 120 meters, and then whirled back to 49—and the plug of mud which had stopped up the opening of the manometer from without was instantly blown away with a whiff of compressed air.

We also cleared all the exhaust pipes outside through the application of compressed air. They had become clogged with slime, which had been stirred up by our dizzy dance. Then the exhaust pumps began to drone in their good old fashion and obediently the *Deutschland* went soaring toward the surface.

We had lain along the bottom over an hour and a half.

Captain Hinsch came alongside in the *Timmins*. He was vastly relieved. He had been unable to account for our long submersion, and had been greatly troubled about us. We must have blundered into a kind of pit, in which the sand "ground," as in a mill, and into which we had gradually burrowed through the circular movements which had stirred up the slime and the mud. I now stationed the *Timmins* at two miles distance, so that she might observe one final and important trial dive.

I desired to rise to the surface without moving forward, so that only the periscope would appear above the surface. This is not so easy as it sounds. When the submarine ascends under power with the aid of the diving rudders, it is, of course, much easier to assume a certain position, but in this case the periscopes draw a small wake of foam along the surface and this, under certain circumstances, might prove most treacherous.

We therefore made the attempt to rise from a greater depth by means of balancing and by exhausting and refilling the tanks, in order to float in such a position as merely to show our periscopes above water and absolutely vertical.

The attempt was successful. We managed to protude our periscope feelers without attracting the notice of the *Timmins* which knew, of course, about where we were lying. It was only after the turret had emerged that she saw us.

I now had the certainty that we were prepared for all eventualities and might attempt to break through without being observed. So we proceeded quietly upon our course, accompanied by the *Timmins*. Just before the coming of dusk, we reached the opening between the two capes.

XII

BREAKING THROUGH

THE night had already come as we approached the dangerous region. In front of us sparkled the fixed beacon on Cape Henry, while upon our port Cape Charles sent its lightnings through the darkness at brief intervals. At the apex of this triangle, we proceeded quietly toward the momentous division.

Suddenly two searchlights upon our starboard flashed across the water. The infernal beams of light ran madly, searching across the dark floods. Mechanically I counted a few seconds. Then the core of the light pierced full into my eyes. . . .

[183]

There was no longer time to dive, and the betraying glare remained fixed upon the *Deutschland.*

We two men upon the turret looked at each other for a moment. In this beautiful free illumination our expressions were quite visible.

Then we saw the two beams of the searchlight, after they had ascertained our presence, sweep twice toward the zenith and suddenly go out. After we had once more accustomed our eyes to the darkness, we discovered two dark craft upon our starboard. They looked like fishing trawlers.

"The damned villains!" I heard Krapohl murmur at my side. "They have betrayed us!"

I am sorry to say that he was right.

For the shaft of a mighty searchlight now rose vertically into the air, obviously as a signal for the English cruisers waiting outside.

I knew that it was now or never.

I gave the command: "Clear ship for diving! Submerge to 18 meters."

We at once took our course toward the south.

After half an hour we emerged again, as I wished once more to get my exact bearings. Wr. scarcely had time, however, to cast a look around, before we were forced to evade a threatening danger by a rapid dive. For hardly two hundred yards across our bows, we saw the patroling American armored cruiser come rushing on.

The cruiser had also seen these conspicuous light signals and had come to keep an eye on proceedings along the American three-mile limit. According to the newspaper reports, this armored

cruiser had aeroplanes aboard and had
been ordered to carry out certain naval
exercises in Chesapeake Bay. I am
nevertheless inclined to the opinion
that the American Government had ordered the vessel to patrol the three-
mile limit in order to observe what
happened when we made for the sea.
I am also personally firmly convinced
that the splendid spirit which pre-
vails among the officers and crew of
the American Navy would have resulted in this cruiser taking energetic
action against any violation of the international limits, and not contented
itself with mere observation.

That such a violation was not by any
means impossible, and that it was prevented upon this memorable night
merely by the resolute attitude of this
American warship, appears the more

probable from the following circumstance: Some days before our departure, an English cruiser had passed Cape Henry at night during a fog, had gone searching about the whole of Chesapeake Bay in the most shameless manner, and then, without disclosing its identity, had steamed away.

In the meantime, we had forced our boat into the depths with a great list forward. We rose to the surface only after the rumble of the screws of the American vessel had died away in the distance.

We knew that the most dangerous moment of our entire voyage was now approaching. We once more marked our exact position, and then proceeded to make all the preparations necessary for our breaking through.

Then we dived and drove forward.

All our senses were keyed to the utmost, our nerves taut to the breaking-point with that cold excitement which sends quivers through one's soul, the while outwardly one remains quite serene, governed by that clear and icy deliberation which is apt to possess a man who is fully conscious of the unknown perils toward which he goes. . . .

We knew our path. We had already been informed that fishermen had been hired to spread their nets along certain stretches of the three-mile limit; nets in which we were supposed to entangle ourselves; nets into which devilish mines had very likely been woven. . . .

Possibly these nets were merely attached to buoys which we were then supposed to drag along after us, thus betraying our position. . . .

We were prepared for all emergencies, so that in case of extreme necessity we should be able to free ourselves of the nets. But all went well.

It was a dark night. Quietly and peacefully the lighthouses upon the two capes sent forth their light, the while a few miles further out death lay lowering for us in every imaginable form.

But while the English ships were racing up and down, jerking their searchlights across the waters and searching again and again in every imaginable spot, they little surmised that, at times within the radius of their own shadows, a periscope pursued its silent way, and under this periscope—the *U-Deutschland.*

That night at twelve o'clock, after

hours of indescribable tension, I gave the command to rise.

We Had Broken Through!

Slowly the *Deutschland* rose to the surface, the tanks were blown out and the Diesel engines flung into their gearing. At our highest speed we now went rushing toward the free Atlantic. Behind us to the northwest the Britishers were still searching the waters with whole sheaves of search-lights. I dare say they must have got very nervous toward the end.

XIII

HOMEWARD BOUND

NEVER before had the *Deutschland* traveled at such speed as during those early morning hours of the 3rd of August. She swept onward in a wonderful way, flinging up a broad strip of foam to either side. The engines chanted in most beautiful harmony; the combustion was perfect and there was not the slightest vapor visible at the exhausts, so that even Mr. Kissling himself was highly satisfied, and almost went so far in an access of unconscious tenderness as to stroke the rods of his beloved motors.

When the sun rose, the coast had long since vanished in the gray mist,

and there was not a single craft visible.
We remained on the surface and went
rushing on like the very devil! Ah!
for how much we have to thank our
engines. When we reached Baltimore,
after our long arduous trip they were
still in the best of condition. Not a
single repair was necessary and we
might have started on the return trip
at once without overhauling. Nor must
it be forgotten that our engines were
forced to work under the most extraordinary conditions, conditions such as
those resulting from the dreadful temperature in the Gulf Stream which
made the most unexpected demands
upon the entire *materiel*. It may be
calmly asserted that never before have
oil motors had to undergo a working
test under an outer temperature of
53° *Celsius*. These things, of course,

WELCOMING THE CREW OF THE "DEUTSCHLAND" AT THE CITY HALL IN BREMEN

CAPTAIN KÖNIG AND DR. ALFRED LOHMANN, PRESI-
DENT OF THE GERMAN OCEAN NAVIGATION CO.,
LEAVING RECEPTION GIVEN CAPTAIN
KÖNIG IN BREMEN

could not be foreseen when our special type of engine was built, and that they never once went on strike, nor developed the slightest engine trouble, constitutes the most perfect proof of their magnificent construction and material.

So we went plunging along, and all too soon we once more found ourselves in the hot, humid atmosphere and turbid air of the Gulf Stream. We were once more in the thick of its beautiful characteristics and the accompanying phenomena. We were once more treated to sultry dampness and electrically laden air, to an excited sea, to battened-down hatches and infernal heat. And the old Stream did not even consent to shove us, as we certainly had the right to expect.

But all these hardships we bore with

a cheerful spirit, for the danger-zone lay behind us and we were homeward bound. The high seas also dwindled away the closer we approached the limits of the Gulf Stream.

On the evening of the second day it already became possible to open all the hatches on the deck, but we had hardly begun to enjoy the fresh, pure air which was to make our stay beneath decks endurable, than there came the sudden command: "Cover hatches and dive!"

A steamer had come up and had approached us so closely and along the lines of our own course that we were no longer able to evade it above water.

When we climbed to the surface an hour later, the night had come, and we experienced a most marvellous natural phenomena, a sea-illumination of

dæmonian unreality. We had gone
down into the depths during a quiet
sea and in dark water, but on rising
we emerged in a sea of flame. A phos-
phorescent glow now possessed the sea,
of an intensity and radiance such as
I had never before experienced in all
my life; and such as is possible only
upon the outer confines of the Gulf
Stream.

When we were still some four yards
under the surface, during our ascent,
it seemed as if we were working up
through an incandescent medium of
luminous transparency. Shortly before the turret emerged from the water,
I had cast a glance aft, and seen the
entire body of the ship, from the stern
on, slipping like a great dark shuttle
through this flaming element. The
screws cast up whirlpools of flame,

and the entire movement of the vessel roused the surrounding waters to a still fiercer phosphorescence, an intensive flaming-up and a darting of sparks and strips of fire.

A fresh breeze had set in. It flung the ecstatic waters in luminous spheroids, and a coruscating rain across the entire deck. Wherever the eye rested upon the surface of the sea it saw nothing but a tossing world of lambent waves, through which our vessel ploughed a fiery furrow.

We stood as if under the ban of wizardry. The magic splendor of the vision increased as the wind and the sea grew stronger.

All the men not on duty came up and stared at the fairy spectacle, taking no notice of the seas which already had begun to sweep over the deck. Many of them were soaked to the skin.

"Fire it may be, but it puts out a man's pipe," remarked our gigantic boatswain, Humke. A spurt of brine had extinguished his pipe for the third time, so that he now determined to protect his beloved cutty by stowing it in his pocket.

The "fire" grew wetter and wetter, and in another half hour only the officer of the watch and the lookout remained on the turret.

After we had left the Gulf Stream, we encountered a stiff northwester and a heavy sea until we once more ran into fair weather. On one of these evenings, First Officer Krapohl was standing watch with Humke upon the turret, and ceaselessly sweeping the horizon with the glass. The paling heavens had already merged into the dusky reaches of the sea.

"Light ahead!" Humke suddenly announced.

"I've already seen that star myself," remarked the officer quietly, letting the glass sink.

"Well, I dunno, Herr Krapohl, but that ain't no star," replied our good sailorman.

The two thereupon reported to me, and I ascended the turret, full of expectation. I took the glass, looked, and then laughed.

"Humke, you are mistaken."

For, fairly high above the horizon, I saw a faint, white light which, had it belonged to a ship, would already have stood too high above the sea-level, judging by its degree of luminosity.

Our boatswain, however, insisted upon his own opinion.

"Beggin' your pardon, Cap'n, it ain't a star."

I handed the glass to Humke, but he at once put it down again, and remarked:

"A man can't see well with them there things."

He then contracted his brows, sent another piercing glance toward the light, and said, with deep conviction:

"All the same, it ain't a star, it's a light."

We kept the thing under very sharp observation. At length I began to see through the glass a red glow growing visible beside the white light. We now knew that a steamer was coming toward us.

I at first took it to be a small vessel, the more so as at first the height of the two lights was not greatly differentiated—that is to say, the red portlight of the steamer was hung not very far below the white light. Soon after, however, I was surprised to see how quickly the red light ranged outward, or rather how quickly the interval of space between the two lights appeared to increase.

There was only one conclusion possible—the vessel was approaching us at a most extraordinary speed.

While I was still deliberating over this point, and already thinking of a swift destroyer, I discovered, at a comparatively great distance, behind the two lights, something that looked like a white, moving glow, or a feebly illuminated wave.

We were unable to make out what

this might mean. It was obvious that this wave must belong to the lights, for it came on at the same speed. And we were right, for it did not take long before we saw trembling in the glass like some dim foreboding the gigantic outlines of a huge steamer, which, with mighty upper works, came rushing on through the darkness. The white glow was merely its wake which, true to the colossal proportions of the ship, became visible only at a considerable distance from the ship's lanterns.

We kept staring for a few moments longer and discovered four towering smoke-stacks. We were now certain that this was a large Cunarder, which was roaring along with masked lights, merely carrying a top-light and the side-lights.

It was really a most spectral apparition. The dark and powerful vessel
went chasing on through the night, and
it was not necessary to be particularly romantic in order to think of
the Flying Dutchman. Our good
Humke expressed his feelings in the
words:

"My, what a buster!"

"Full speed ahead and rudder hard
to starboard."

We thus left the course of the proud
Cunarder. All the men of the off-watch
came up on deck in order to have a
peep at the spectacle.

In spite of the most vigilant lookout, we saw absolutely nothing during
the next few days. The weather like-
wise remained fair, and so our return
home, even more than our outward
voyage, began to assume the character

of a peaceful, uneventful mercantile voyage.

We now seemed for the first time to be able to enjoy the convenient and practical inner arrangement of the boat, the cabins, and our cheerful little mess-room. How often, as we sat about the table in the mess-room and set the gramophone going, did we feel a sudden gratitude toward the men who had not only given the ship her seaworthy form, but also devised all the many little conveniences which permitted us to lead a quite tolerable life even below the levels of the sea.

When our worthy and flaxen-haired steward, Stucke, always with the same solemn expression upon his honest face, always looking a little astonished, would place a bottle of Californian claret before us, while we were lying "somewhere" along the bottom of the sea, with a vigorous Channel wind blowing many meters over our heads—strange thoughts were ours. It required no particular fantasy to imagine ourselves the successors of Captain Nemo, who, in an extremely modern *Nautilus* were able to descend to all depths and to deliver a stinging blow against the injustice and rank arrogance of a certain people—provided, of course, that one had read Jules Verne.

For I must at last make a confession, something which, up to now, I had kept locked as a fearful secret in my breast. It was only as the commander of a submarine merchant vessel, upon my return from America, that I was able to make good a serious deficiency in my education. That which

I had neglected in my youth I was able to take up only now at the age of 49 years. For the first time, in the hull of the *U-Deutschland* it was decreed that I make myself acquainted with Jules Verne.

It was due to the courtesy and attentiveness of an American friend that I had at Baltimore become the recipient of a book; a book—how shall I express myself?—intended as a spur to incentive, to emulation. The book bore the title:

"Twenty Thousand Leagues Under the Sea. For Young People."

I read it with interest.

The other events that transpired upon our homeward voyage are soon told. We proceeded calmly and peacefully upon our way. We evaded several steamers at a greater distance, by making a détour upon the surface, which gradually made us experts in this matter. The weather was, for the most part, good. Once there was fog and a smooth sea.

One afternoon, as I sat at the desk in my cabin in order to work, I heard from the neighboring central a command given by the helmsman. It was "Starboard, 20," and was repeated. Immediately afterwards came the command: "Port, 10," which induced me to hurry on deck before I received the report of the officer on watch.

Here a singular spectacle presented itself. Everywhere, as far as the eye could reach, the sea was covered with a field of black oil-barrels, through which we were forced to worm our way.

The first glimpse of these black and eerie things, bobbing up and down upon the waves, made one think of a mine-field, but the characteristic form of the barrels and their contents, which had partly distributed itself over the water, gave ample testimony of their harmless-ness. We were, nevertheless, obliged to exercise considerable caution in steering through this remarkable plan-tation, but the field was too vast for us to avoid without a consider-able loss of time. The number of barrels which came within the circle of our vision we estimated as at least 1,000.

"This is fine practice," exclaimed Krapohl, "for the elegant movements we shall be obliged to make later, when we go snaking our way through the English mine-fields. I think we might risk the return passage through the English Channel.''

So we went zigzagging on at half speed to port, then to starboard, then to port, for over an hour. We also saw wrack from a ship, so that we assumed that some steamer had met with a disaster or been blown up.

We now approached once more the sphere of the English patrol-boats. The lookouts were doubled and all hands stood at the diving-stations. Now and again we saw vessels whose vigilance we escaped by diving or a change of course. One war vessel, apparently a small English cruiser, we cheated out of the possibility of even seeing us by a swift dive. After proceeding under water for an hour, we once more rose toward the surface, only to have the periscope reveal to us

CELEBRATION AT CITY HALL, BREMEN,
AUGUST 25, 1916

The crowd in front numbered many thousands. The officers and crew
on the balcony, acknowledging cheers

PORTRAIT OF OFFICERS AND CREW OF THE
"DEUTSCHLAND"
Taken on their arrival, at the mouth of the Weser,
August 23, 1916

while- still at a depth of 11 meters another English ship. We at once sank to 20 meters, and this game of hide and seek was repeated three times in succession.

Toward noon we climbed to the top for good, blew out the tanks and forged ahead at full speed.

Favored by good weather, we rapidly approached our goal. On an evening in August, about 8 o'clock, we saw a whole circle of white lights surrounding the entire horizon.

I naturally began to fear that we were surrounded. When we turned to starboard, we saw these infernal lights. When we turned to port, they also popped up there.

However, our good Zeiss glasses soon relieved us of the anxiety of falling into a trap at the last moment, almost in view of home. The twilight was still sufficiently clear to enable us to see by the outlines of these sinister vessels that they were in reality nothing more deadly than Dutch herring loggers.

XIV

HOME AGAIN

'A FAVORABLE following wind drove along with us toward home. About six o'clock one August morning, there was once more an alarm. In the far-off distance, something had popped up, something which looked like a boat's sail of a most remarkable form. On approaching closer, this sail revealed itself as the turret of a U-boat, which, with flooded decks, was churning along its way.

Although we were at first inclined to make various edifying and instructive remarks with regard to this peculiar image which presented itself to us from the distance, and to expatiate upon our own appearance at three nautical miles, there was nevertheless something else of far greater moment for us to consider. The question for us was—was this an English or a German submarine?

We preferred, however, in order to make sure of all eventualities, to show as little of ourselves as possible, and to scuttle away beneath at the last moment.

We had already flooded all tanks except No. 3, and the seas were flinging across the decks and splashing against the turret, and the turret itself was already cutting into the green waters, when a well-known signal was hoisted by the submarine and we were reassured of its being German. We at once sent our answer.

And then the command rang out:

"Exhaust with air blast!"

I had never given an order upon the *Deutschland* with a more joyous heart. And never was an order more joyously carried out after I had shouted down into the central: "Hurrah, the first German submarine's in sight!"

What did it matter that we stood upon the turret, still awash with oil and sea-water, or that the spray shot over us—what did it matter? There, across the North Sea, the first greeting of Germany, of our great Fatherland, came rushing on. We forged ahead at full speed. All hands were on deck, and in a short time both vessels lay within calling distance of each other.

The first deafening hurrahs came roaring over to us, and we answered them with equal power.

Then we exchanged greetings and news, after which our paths once more separated—we toward home—*U-X* to its work.

The day drew to its close and the night came down once more.

So we swept onward, without a light on deck, without a light in the turret, like some dark phantom.

Then, on the following morning, as the sun arose, we saw before us in the distance an unmistakable silhouette which glimmered redly through the veils of mist. It was an island, a bulwark in the North Sea. Heligoland lay before us.

Things soon began to grow lively upon the waters. Torpedo-boats came rushing up, vanguard patrols puffed along, flag signals flew into the air, the wireless crackled. Everywhere mes-

sages and greetings came flying toward
us, and then the iron ring of the German fleet which holds its trusty watch
out there upon the seas, closed about
our little *Deutschland.* Under its protection we now steered past Heligoland
toward our own home port. While we
were already approaching the well-
known waters, and before the low
sandy stretches of the home coast came
into view, we were treated to a spectacle of overwhelming magnificence—
a greeting such as had never been on
land or sea—and carried out with the
most amazing dash.

We saw two immense birds lift
themselves from the land. They were
two hydroplanes, which came on at terrific speed and then alighted like two
gigantic water-fowl upon the lightly
heaving swell. They then shot, slightly

skimming the surface of the sea with their floats, to within a stone's throw of the *Deutschland*. Here they made a lightning turn and came rattling past us, turned again and then literally hopped over us, roaring close above our turret with a shouting of hurrahs and a swinging of caps. . . .

Such was our reception by the youngest arm of the German Navy.

Comparisons are odious.

But as we once more neared the German coast, and felt ourselves surrounded by the protecting arm of the German navy, it was impossible for me to help comparing this with our arrival in America.

Surely no one could have been received more heartily nor with greater enthusiasm than we had been by the Americans. An easygoing and carefree people had taken pleasure in a daring, adventurous act, and had expressed its sympathy for an enterprise that was novel and unheard-of, and which called for men.

But here we were more than daring and successful adventurers. Here our own people once more took us to their hearts as peaceful combatants in their glorious struggle. Here was revealed to us the inspiring vision of their power beneath the sea, upon the sea, and in the air. This was to me the significance of that splendid greeting given us by the airmen. This is what I felt when we were convoyed by the patrol boats to the estuary of the Weser, where we cast anchor before the Hohen Weg lighthouse—once more in German ground.

XV

HOW GERMANY WELCOMED US BACK

FROM the roads of Heligoland to the estuary of the Weser we had been welcomed by the navy, but on the voyage up the Weser, and in Bremen, we were welcomed by an entire people.

On the afternoon of August 23d the *Deutschland* had cast anchor at the Weser's mouth. The wires had at once spread the tidings through the entire German Empire, the longed-for tidings which awakened such unbounded joy.

We were surprised and proud to learn that the arrival of the *Deutsch-land* had been made the occasion of a

festal day for the entire German people, and that a reception was preparing
for our little boat along the banks of
the Weser such as had seldom fallen
to the lot of a fortunate ship. Our
journey up the Weser shaped itself
to a triumphal progress beyond all
comparison. Behind the hundreds of
thousands who had come to cheer us
from the banks of the river stood in-
visible millions of the German people,
all imbued with the same emotion.

This expressed itself everywhere in
exuberant manifestations of joy and
pride, by old and young, by high and
low—from the German Kaiser to the
humblest dock-laborer and the tiniest
cabin-boy who waved his little flag in
Bremen and shouted out of sheer delight.

Among all the expressions of ecstatic

joy with which we were deluged, I was particularly moved by one—a stirring poem which was sent to me by Hans Dowidat, Chief Stoker aboard the *Posen,* the day after our arrival:

"U-DEUTSCHLAND"

Das war ein Jubel von Ohr zu Ohr,
Ein deutsches U-Boot in Baltimore,
Ein deutsches U-Boot gefahrumstellt,
Trägt deutsche Waren von Welt zu Welt!
Und wie auch der Brite die Tat verdreht
Und wie sie alle geflucht und geschmäht;
Stolz flatterte dennoch die Flagge empor
Am deutschen U-Boot in Baltimore!

"Good day, Kaptän, woher die Fahrt?"
"Wir kommen von Bremen, sind deutsche Art!"
"Von Deutschland? Well, das nenn' ich kühn,
Ja, liess euch der Brite denn ruhig ziehn?"
"Was kehrt uns Franzen- und Britenlug?
Wir fahren, wo Wasser um unseren Bug,
Wir fahren, wo Wasser um unser Deck
Und wissen von keinem Britenschreck!

Doch ist es dir recht, so machen wir,
Freund Yankee, jetzt ein Geschäft mit dir.
Wir bringen so manches, was Uncle Sam
Schon lange nicht mehr in sein Land bekam."
"Well, das ist gut, ich sage yes;
Denn business bleibt business!"

Da hub sich geschäftiges Leben am Kai,
Gewichtige Kräne rollten herbei,
Die schrien und kreischten und summten dumpf,
Die tauchten hinein in des Schiffes Rumpf
Und hoben die Werte, die deutsche Hand,
Über — und unter das Meer gesandt.
Das war ein Lärmen, das war ein Klang
In Bunker und Zelle, in Last und Tank,
Und draussen das Volk von Amerika,
Staunend das deutsche Wunder sah!—

Leer die Bunker und leer die Last,
Wieder hebt sich lärmende Hast,
Doch der Kran, der nun in das Boot sich taucht,
Trägt fremde Waren, die Deutschland braucht!—

So schafften die Deutschen in Baltimore—
Franzosen, Russen und Briten im Chor
Schwuren mit einem grässlichen Schwur
Niemals lenkt heimwärts das Boot die Spur,

Voyage of the Deutschland

"Wo wir es treffen im Meeresrund,
Muss es mit Mann und Maus auf den Grund!"
Sie haben den Hafen mit Schiffen umsäumt,
Sie haben von köstlichem Fange geträumt,
Sie haben geharrt und haben gewacht,
Sie haben gelauert bei Tag und Nacht
Und hatten nur eins, nur eins im Sinn,
Die "Deutschland" darf nicht nach Deutsch-
    land hin!

Es ging die Zeit, und es kam der Tag,
Da klar zur Reise "U-Deutschland" lag.
Und wie die Hebel auf "Fahrt" gestellt,
Da lauschte mit stockendem Atem die Welt!
All unsre Feinde in West and Ost,
Sie harrten nur einer, nur einer Post:
"Das Boot, das uns so sehr gekränkt,
Liegt auf dem Meeresgrund versenkt!"

Doch die "Deutschland" fuhr und all ihr
    Geschrei,
All ihre Schwüre verflogen wie Spreu.
Die "Deutschland" fuhr, und keine Gewalt
Bot ihrem ruhmreichen Wege halt!
Wohl ging noch oftmals die Sonne auf,
Es richten sich Tage zum Wochenlauf.
Frug mancher sorgend im deutschen Land:
Wann endlich kehrt sie zum Heimatstrand?

Voyage of the Deutschland

Und nun kam der Tag, und nun fliegt das Wort
Durch hundert Millionen Kehlen fort,
Das Wort, das nimmer verklingt und verjährt:
" 'U-Deutschland,' 'U-Deutschland' ist heimge-
kehrt!''
>   HANS DOWIDAT,
>   *Oberheizer auf S. M. S. "Posen."*
>   *Wohnschiff "Ägir."*

Early on the morning of August 25th
the *Deutschland* began her pageant-
like progress up the Weser. The rain
came down in streams, but nothing
was able to disturb the general air of
jubilation as we went on our way, accompanied by a convoy of steamers,
and our masts and turret decorated
with flowers. Toward 8 o'clock in the
morning we arrived in the roadstead
of Bremerhaven.

Dun-colored clouds hung low in the
skies and let fall their heavy showers
upon the thousands who stood along

the dykes or came to meet us on steamers, lighters, launches and in rowboats.

Thunderous hurrahs came echoing to us from the city, and the chime of bells mingled with these shouts and cheers. But high over everything else we heard the strains of the song "Deutschland, Deutschland über Alles." That song was precisely 75 years old upon this day.

We took a Weser pilot aboard and continued on our way. In Nordenham, Brake and Blumenthal we were greeted with flags, with crashing salvoes of guns—factories and steam sirens sent up their roaring salutes. The Lloyd steamers bid us welcome and flag-wagged us their felicitations for which we thanked them in like fashion. We passed Vegesack. The

INTERIOR VIEW OF THE "DEUTSCHLAND"

The central control or navigating room

THE "DEUTSCHLAND" ON THE STOCKS
Photograph taken the day before the launching

work at the Vulcan Docks was standing still, and hundreds of workmen
crowded the quays. Their thunderous
hurrahs greeted us, and from now on
our advance became more and more
triumphal. The population of Vegesack stood assembled along the piers
and the river banks. Here too, there
was music and song, a thunder of guns
and a storm of cheers. The ranks grew
steadily denser the nearer the ship approached its home haven. Shortly before noon we reached Lankenau, whose
lagoon seemed crowded with all the
inhabitants of Bremen, who seemed to
have chosen it as a coign of vantage.
We saw the people, a veritable sea of
heads, waving their hats, umbrellas
and handkerchiefs. The spectacle was
simply indescribable, this apparently
endless multitude, these thousands

15 [225]

upon thousands, like a black and liv-
ing sea across which there passed a
tidal motion of waving umbrellas, glimmering white muslin and hands, hands,
hands. . . .

Precisely at noon the *Deutschland*
entered the free harbor and made fast
to the pier, which was decorated in
festal manner.

Here the Grand Duke of Oldenburg,
Representatives of the Senate, and the
citizens, and of the military and civic
authorities—among them Count Zeppelin—were assembled to receive us.

As soon as the ship was made fast,
I ordered the crew on deck. Herr
Alfred Lohmann, the founder and
president of the Deutsche Reederei
Gesellschaft, greeted us as follows:

"Your Highness! Your Magnificence! Your Excellencies! Gentle-

men! At this historical moment, which marks the return of the world's first submarine, after covering 8,500 nautical miles, I welcome to their home haven our *Deutschland* and her gallant crew. I welcome them, not only in the name of our Company, but in the name of the entire German nation.

"She stole out of the Weser, her existence known only to a trusted few, she crept through and underneath the English fleet, and on the 10th of July she brought her valuable cargo of dye-stuffs safe into Baltimore. Her arrival was a surprise to the whole world. Only a short time before her appearance even shipping experts had pronounced such an undertaking to be impossible.

"It was particularly agreeable to me to be assured of the warm interest and satisfaction with which the *Deutschland's* arrival in America was greeted by all true Americans—that is to say, by all Americans possessed of the free spirit of Washington and Franklin, all whose judgment had not been warped by subservience to the English mammon.

"Our Company takes pride in the thought that it has succeeded, in the very midst of war, in sending dyestuffs to America under the German flag. America herself, on the contrary, is not even able to secure the immunity of her post from Europe. I shall not mention the many other breaches of international and naval law committed against the neutrals, and especially the smaller nations, by our enemies.

"Yes, the crew of the *Deutschland* have done a great work. If the ship gave no warning of her setting-out, none the less her departure from Baltimore was openly announced. 'It was like a triumphal procession,' wrote Havas. 'It was a symbol of freedom,' we Germans think, dreaming of the 'Right of the Nations to the Freedom of the Seas.'

"Our enemies could not hinder the *Deutschland's* departure from Chesapeake Bay, and a blockade of the North Sea did not exist for her. The goods which lie before us at this moment, goods worth many millions of marks, all brought from America by the *Deutschland,* are sufficient proof of that.

"The officers and crew have performed a feat of seamanship which is worthy of our Hanseatic forefathers! The news of the return of the *Deutsch-*

land has been received with the liveliest joy in all the states of the German Empire, and in the countries of our faithful allies. But especially deep is the feeling of our brothers out in the trenches and in the Navy.

"The Company has awaited this return with an absolute confidence in the ability, the foresight and the sense of duty of the *Deutschland's* crew. After these trying weeks of close confinement to this little ship, always face to face with ruthless enemies, I bid them all a hearty welcome home.

"And I give expression to the gratitude we feel by calling for three cheers for the *Deutschland,* her Commander, Captain König, the officers and the crew! Hurrah! hurrah! hurrah!"

I answered with a short: "Long live the Senate and the citizenry of the

Free Hansa City of Bremen''—lustily supported by my men.

Patriotic airs came to us from a neighboring Lloyd steamer, the *Frankfurt*—after which we went on land and were presented one after the other to the guests of honor. The reception was simple and dignified, and therefore the more edifying.

After overcoming a distance of some 8,450 nautical miles, of which not more than 190 were covered under water, the first of all merchant submarines had come back to its native port. The *U-Deutschland's* voyage to America was over.

On the evening of this memorable day, a big state banquet took place in the old Rathaus at Bremen. It was given by the Senate of the City in celebration of the return of the *Deutschland.* The speeches made upon this occasion give a brief outline of the circumstances which led to the building of the *Deutschland.* It will therefore prove interesting to quote them here.

Burgomaster Dr. Barkhausen had bidden the guests welcome with hospitable words, had communicated a resolution of the Senate to the effect that a special medal was to be struck in commemoration of this day, and had toasted the Deutsche Ocean Reederei and the crew of the *Deutschland.*

In the name of the Reederei, or Shipowners, their President, Dr. A. Lohmann, now replied as follows:

"Your Magnificence, your Excellencies, gentlemen! In the name of the

Commander of the *Deutschland,* Captain König, and his officers and crew, I express profound thanks to the high Senate, adding to them those of our Company, for the high honor which the Senate has bestowed upon the crew of the *Deutschland,* by means of the medal which is to serve as a memento of this peaceful achievement of commerce in the midst of war. For the appreciative words regarding the activities of my co-workers and myself, I express my deepest thanks to your Magnificence. Since the beginning of the war, I have gladly and willingly devoted my activities to the welfare of the State. The conviction that our splendid people, despite the overwhelming forces of their enemies, were not to be conquered in this war which they are waging for the sake of their national independence and freedom, the conviction that the spiritual forces and the trust which animates our entire people, that the thorough training undergone since the Wars of Liberation, and the natural devotion of duty which has been inherited by every German, could never be overborne, has been the guiding motive in all my work. And everywhere did I find trusting fellow workers who thought as I did.

"I therefore wish to express my thanks to all these collaborators of mine. My special gratitude is due to Director Stapelfeldt and to my colleague, Director-General Heineken and Commercial Councillor Herrmann.

"The Deutsche Ocean Reederei, as already alluded to by Your Magnificence, was founded in all secrecy. Its task was to lie entirely in the transportation of goods of the highest value. It was necessary to purchase the raw materials in America with the utmost caution, to store them safely, to secure a safe anchorage for the *Deutschland,* and protect her from all attacks. This was done in the most admirable way by Mr. Paul G. L. Hilken and his father, as well as Captain Hinsch and his assistants. The part played by Captain König, his officers and crew, in this project, has already been conveyed to your Magnificence. I, for my part, speaking in the name of the Company, once more wish to express my thanks to my co-workers upon the *Deutschland.* It will interest you, gentlemen, to learn something concerning the history of the Deutsche Ocean Reederei, and of the evolution of the *Deutsch-*

land, the *Bremen,* and their still un-named sister ship.

"When, in September, 1915, it became clear that, in spite of all the successes of the Central Powers, the war would very likely last for months longer, it became apparent that the question of supplying Germany with rubber and metals might become a burning one. I therefore consulted with the 'Weser' stock company, after having had an interview with a promi-nent expert in shipbuilding. The 'Weser' Company expressed itself as ready to draw up plans for a subma-rine of about 500 tons capacity. These plans were delivered to me on the 3rd of October; a period of building was estimated at eleven months—deliver-able on the 1st of September, 1916, since the motors would first have to be built. It was apparent that we should have to make an effort to attain our goal somewhat earlier. Almost simultaneously, and without our knowledge, the Germania Docks of Kiel submitted to their parent house, the Frederick Krupp Co., plans for the construction of a submarine of some 700 tons freight capacity—this about the beginning of October.

"The Germania yard wished to deliver the first boat in the short time of six months—that is to say, in April. Both these plans expressed absolute assurance in the feasibility of the idea. I would like to compare this conjunction with a happy marriage, in which the same thought animates the man and the woman. The docks were the mother which gave birth to the child; the father was the company, which was

[237]

to lead the child forth into the world. The soul and spirit of this infant enterprise were evidenced through our Captain, his officers and crew, who have fulfilled this splendid achievement of taking the *Deutschland* to America and back.

"On the 15th of October, we came to terms, and the two boats were given by the Syndicate to the Germania docks to build. The *Deutschland* was delivered at the beginning of April. It is a brilliant masterpiece of the Germania docks and, as we are accustomed to expect in all work that bears the name of Frederick Krupp, perfect in its execution. Captain König was able to report from America that all was in perfect order after his 4,000-mile trip. The same applies to his report made upon his arrival at Bremen.

"This co-operation between spirit and force, this utilization of all the new and scientific inventions, as well as an elevated sense of duty are the factors that have made the Germania Docks great. To-day when the *Deutschland* has returned to us, we stand face to face with a new achievement in the art of shipbuilding, and for this, too, the German people give thanks to this enterprise. I trust that you will give expression to this feeling by three cheers in honor of the Germania Docks."

After the next course, Director Zetzmann, of the Germania Docks, made the following speech:

"Your Magnificence, your Excellencies, gentlemen! I have the honor to express my heartiest thanks to the

Senate—in the name of the Germania Docks—for the privilege of participating in this festival. I also wish to express my thanks to my predecessor, Dr. Alfred Lohmann, for the kind things he has said of my firm, in whose name I thank him. Herr Lohmann has told you many interesting things regarding the evolution of his company. Permit me to give you a few facts from the workshops in which the *Deutschland* and the *Bremen* originated. It was not easy to come to the conclusion to undertake the building of such a boat, not because we feared the mechanical difficulties, but because we scarcely ventured to risk tasking our construction bureaus still further, burdened as they already were with war contracts.

"We at first proceeded to work along

the models of the war submarines, thinking this would lessen the labor of construction. We discovered, however, that this did not lead to the desired results as far as cargo capacity and storage room were concerned. We had to proceed on more radical lines—not to develop a freighter from a cruiser—but to create a new type of freighter.

"Our constructors now went to work with a fiery enthusiasm, and the plans were soon ready. . . . Herr Krupp von Bohlen declared that a boat of this type could be built and should be built in the shortest possible time, so the Germania Docks were ordered to begin work at once. There were, of course, various inevitable delays. About the middle of October, 1915, we first came in touch with **Dr. Alfred Lohmann**. From that meeting resulted

the marriage which he has described—
war-nuptials as swift as any that the
present time has produced. I have but
one more thing to say—if we were able
to complete this boat in so short a time,
it is owing, not only to the head firm,
but to all sub-contractors as well.
Builders, owners and crews of the
ships, all worked harmoniously together. The trial trips went off
smoothly. We saw the ship set out
upon her trial voyage with the greatest
confidence. Our faith has been glori-
ously justified. May many such successful voyages be carried out by the
Deutschland and her sister ships for
the welfare of our beloved Fatherland
and the fame of the venerable Hansa
city of Bremen!

"To-day's festival will remain a life-
long memory to all who have taken

part in it. . . . When the new portion
of the Rathaus has become as venerable as the old, men will relate to each
other that the lucky voyage of the first
merchant submarine in the world was
celebrated within these walls. . . ."

There had been no announcement of
a public celebration in the market-
place, but in the evening, the crowd,
following its own instinct, streamed
toward this center. People of all
classes were represented, and when the
Bremen military band took up a position on the steps of the Exchange and
began to play the place was quite full.
A more charming celebration could
not be imagined than that which now
began. The patriotic feelings of the
multitude continually reached a pitch
where they could only find relief in

song. Here and there a voice would strike up and at once the whole assembly would fall in.

Again and again the cries rang forth: "Lohmann! Zeppelin! König!" So that we were obliged to obey the voice of the people, and stepped out on the balcony with the crew.

We were met with a hurricane of cheers. The multitude joined in the toast to the Kaiser which I proposed. To the joy of all, Count Zeppelin took up the word and spoke in short, powerful sentences, audible for a long distance. In a voice as clear as that of a young man, he said:

"Deutschland, Deutschland über alles! Three cheers for Bremen and her sons! What shall I say to you? When one sees the feeling which animates the German people, one cannot doubt that the victory will be ours! Hurrah!"

These words called forth unbounded rejoicing, as well as those which I spoke in full confidence:

"We got through!—we always get through! It is our duty to conquer the English with our U-boats and to hold out."

In answer to the universal demand, Dr. Lohmann himself finally stepped to the railing of the balcony and devoted a few pithy words to the services rendered by Count Zeppelin—and your humble servant.

After Dr. Lohmann's speech, the band played the hymn of thanksgiving, "Wir treten mit Beten vor Gott den Gerechten" (To the God of Justice we offer our prayers), which was sung by everybody.

Meanwhile, darkness had fallen, and in the glow of the electric lights, the market place, as seen from the old Rathaus, itself streaming with light, presented a wonderful spectacle. No one wanted to bring this delightful celebration to an end. The singing continued indefatigably. Then Burgomaster Dr. Barkhausen, the President of the Senate, rose to speak. He said:

"We have assembled here to ratify once more our determination that the spirit which has been with the *Deutschland* on her voyage, the spirit of the German people, the spirit which will lead us to victory, shall never die. As a fitting close to this wonderful evening, I once more cry: 'Deutschland, Deutschland über alles! Long live Kaiser and Empire!'"

The words were again received with

enthusiasm. But the gentle hint that it was time to bring the festivities to an end went as yet unheeded.

Once more I was forced to address the crowd. I made it short and sweet; direct from the heart—

"Good night! I am dreadfully tired!"

And so ended this unforgettable day in the history of Germany and of Bremen.